# Student Financial Aid and Women:
## Equity Dilemma?

*by Mary Moran*

*ASHE-ERIC Higher Education Report No. 5, 1986*

*Prepared by*

 ® *Clearinghouse on Higher Education*
*The George Washington University*

*Published by*

*Association for the Study of Higher Education*

*Jonathan D. Fife,*
*Series Editor*

**Cite as**
Moran, Mary. *Student Financial Aid and Women: Equity Dilemma?* ASHE-ERIC Higher Education Report No. 5. Washington, D.C.: Association for the Study of Higher Education, 1986.

*Cover design by Michael David Brown, Inc., Rockville, MD.*

The ERIC Clearinghouse on Higher Education invites individuals to submit proposals for writing monographs for the Higher Education Report series. Proposals must include:
1. A detailed manuscript proposal of not more than five pages.
2. A 75-word summary to be used by several review committees for the initial screening and rating of each proposal.
3. A vita.
4. A writing sample.

**Library of Congress Catalog Card Number 86-72856**
**ISSN 0884-0040**
**ISBN 0-913317-32-2**

ERIC® **Clearinghouse on Higher Education**
The George Washington University
One Dupont Circle, Suite 630
Washington, D.C. 20036

ASHE **Association for the Study of Higher Education**
One Dupont Circle, Suite 630
Washington, D.C. 20036

*Office of Educational*
*Research and Improvement*
*U.S. Department of Education*

This publication was partially prepared with funding from the Office of Educational Research and Improvement, U.S. Department of Education, under contract no. 400-86-0017. The opinions expressed in this report do not necessarily reflect the positions or policies of OERI or the Department. This report was written by Mary Moran in her private capacity. No official support or endorsement by the Department of Education is intended or should be inferred.

# EXECUTIVE SUMMARY

Equal opportunity continues to be an essential variable in justifying the existence of student aid programs, but not much attention has been focused on the degree to which this objective is being achieved for women. While it is no longer news that women are allowed to enroll in prestigious law schools, to play in college sports, and to enroll in nontraditional careers, the question now becomes whether or not women are able to pay for higher education. Who pays? Who benefits? Who should pay? The questions continue to be relevant in the late 1980s, but the answers have shifted since the 1970s.

Although intentional discrimination is generally not the case, significant policy issues exist for women—in total resources available to pay college costs, in the amounts and percentages derived from different sources, and in the way financial aid is distributed among students (Davis 1977; Rosenfeld and Hearn 1982). For every dollar a man receives, a woman receives 68 cents in college earnings, 73 cents in grants, and 84 cents in loans for low-income undergraduates (U.S. Department of Education 1983). The more significant differences between genders appear in discretionary programs like college work, academic merit scholarships, research assistantships, and corporate benefit programs that pay tuition. Because many student aid programs are based on formulas, a necessary unit of analysis becomes the formula itself and other regulatory policies.

Despite the fact that the value and worth of higher education are occasionally challenged, actual statistics on poverty rates, hourly wages, and lifetime earnings make it clear that increased years of schooling are especially important for women. Two out of every three adults in poverty are women, yet poverty rates decrease with additional years of education and salaries become more comparable with increased years of schooling. The income of women with five years or more of college is 66 percent of comparable males with the same level of educational achievement; women with a high school diploma earn 59 percent of the income of similar males.

As the costs of attending college increase at more than double the rate of inflation, the financial concerns of women need to be addressed. Demographic changes continue to affect patterns of college enrollment. Since 1970, college enrollment of women increased 77 percent, compared to a 23 percent increase for men. Indeed, women are contributing to a whole new style of postsecondary education emerging in America. Their patterns of enrollment and economic profiles differ from those of men, however, which should send warning signals to student aid analysts and college officials. Women, for example, far surpass men as adult, part-time, independent, and unclassified students—those categories most likely to present barriers to participating in most financial aid programs. Women tend to depend on low-cost institutions, outnumbering men in public undergraduate four-year and two-year colleges, while men outnumber women in high-cost, private institutions. Further, females with degrees are more likely to enter the careers paying the lowest salaries.

### What Are Major Policy Issues on Student Aid Affecting Women?

Nearly all of the debate, research, and lobbying on student aid have concentrated on percentages of funds received by type of institution—four-year public, two-year public, independent, and proprietary (Miller 1984). Yet some of the more difficult questions are being overlooked: What is the distribution of aid among women? What is the nature of their aid packages? How do women fare in student employment programs? Do women receive equal institutionally funded and corporate-funded aid? What is the nature of their cumulative debt? With over $21 billion invested each year in all forms of student aid, these questions need to be addressed. Several policies are of significant concern:

- The average salary of women repaying Guaranteed Student Loans is $17,407, while that of males is $23,093; thus, women must use a larger proportion of income than men to repay student loans (Boyd and Martin 1986).
- Women are more likely to default on student loans and more likely to declare bankruptcy. Divorced women, for example, are nearly three times as likely to declare bankruptcy as divorced males (17 percent versus 6 percent) (Stanley and Girth 1971).
- In the current push for educational excellence, institutions are intensifying recruiting efforts by awarding scholarships for "academic merit"; women, however,

are underrepresented in such programs and may be confronting unintentional biased attitudes during nomination, screening, and selection. Although female high school seniors, for example, far outnumber males in entering college, 2,280 females and 3,741 males won National Merit Scholarships in 1985, of which 49 females and 264 males received awards in computer sciences.

- Single women with children have the most critical unmet need under current student aid policies. Independent students with children are more than twice as likely to be female and nearly five times as likely to be 24 years of age or older (Fenske, Hearn, and Curry 1985).
- Women are twice as likely as men to be classified as independent students (66 percent versus 34 percent) at the freshman level, have greater unmet financial need, have higher dropout rates, and pay a greater portion of their own college costs than dependent students.
- Working women confront barriers in corporate benefit programs that pay tuition. When employees move into top management positions, their job descriptions usually become more generalized, therefore affording access to a wider range of "job-related" training courses. More women tend to work in nonmanagerial positions with more restricted job descriptions and therefore have fewer such opportunities.
- Child care is a significant cost of attending college for many women, yet student aid policies usually are inconsistent, unclear, or nonexistent about what allowances may be claimed.
- Individuals eligible to receive public assistance, three-fourths of whom are women, generally are required to report all forms of student financial assistance, including student loans, as a "source of income," and that amount is subtracted either in whole or in prorated amounts from total allowable benefits (Hansen and Franklin 1984).
- Low-income females tend to participate at *half* the rate of low-income males in the Guaranteed Student Loan program. More women may be unwilling to apply for loans when they face the prospect of low earnings upon graduation.

- For nearly 65 percent of freshmen women (47 percent of freshmen men), parental aid is a major source of support. Parents of women contribute more than expected compared to amounts contributed by parents of men as a consequence of their receiving less student aid (Davis 1977).
- Men hold disproportionately more research assistantships, as opposed to teaching assistantships. Recipients of research assistantships have more opportunities to publish before they finish their Ph.D.s and receive more subsidized conference travel (Hornig 1983).

### What Actions Are Needed to Improve the Participation of Women in Student Aid Programs?

Given the importance of equal opportunity in achieving educational excellence, the underlying causes of inequity need to be recognized and corrected (Klein 1985; Miller 1984). Several actions could improve women's participation in student aid programs: conducting research, targeting information toward women, funding child care, improving partnerships between high schools and colleges, equalizing pay in college work programs, coordinating requirements for student aid with public assistance offices, increasing student aid from the private sector, reviewing standards of accreditation, expanding options to forgive loans, and implementing self-assessment programs. An overlooked issue in the debate over *Grove City* v. *Bell* is that of equitable distribution of financial assistance for students. Initial interpretations of the ruling have emphasized only the "student aid office," not the "student aid program" as directed by the Supreme Court. This distinction is essential, because many awards of student aid—athletic scholarships, graduate internships, research assistantships, endowments, and scholarships from the private sector—neither filter through nor are reported by the student aid office.

# ADVISORY BOARD

# CONSULTING EDITORS

**Richard Alfred**
Associate Professor and Chair
Graduate Program in Higher and Adult Continuing Education
University of Michigan

**G. Lester Anderson**
Professor Emeritus
Pennsylvania State University

**Robert C. Andringa**
President
Creative Solutions

**John B. Bennett**
Director
Office on Self-Regulation
American Council on Education

**Carole J. Bland**
Associate Professor
Department of Family Practice and Community Health
University of Minnesota

**Judith A. Clementson-Mohr**
Director of Psychological Services
Purdue University

**Mark H. Curtis**
President Emeritus
Association of American Colleges

**Martin Finkelstein**
Associate Professor of Higher Education Administration
Seton Hall University

**Andrew T. Ford**
Provost and Dean of College
Allegheny College

**Timothy Gallineau**
Vice President for Student Development
Saint Bonaventure University

**G. Manuel Gunne**
Adjunct Associate Professor
College of Nursing
University of Utah

**James C. Hearn**
Associate Professor
Department of Educational Policy and Administration
University of Minnesota

**Dennis H. Holmes**
Associate Professor
Department of Education
George Washington University

**Arthur S. Marmaduke**
Director
Eureka Project

**Richard M. Millard**
President
Council on Postsecondary Accreditation

**L. Jackson Newell**
Professor and Dean
University of Utah

**Steven G. Olswang**
Assistant Provost for Academic Affairs
University of Washington

**Patricia Rueckel**
Executive Director
National Association for Women Deans,
   Administrators, and Counselors

**John P. Sciacca**
Assistant Professor
Department of Health, Physical Education, and Recreation
Northern Arizona University

**Richard F. Stevens**
Executive Director
National Association of Student Personnel Administrators

**Thomas R. Wolanin**
Staff Director
Subcommittee on Postsecondary Education
United States House of Representatives

# CONTENTS

**Figure**

**Tables**

# FOREWORD

Education, especially higher education, has long been perceived as the mechanism for upward mobility in America's casteless society, and we have been justifiably proud of the openness of our higher education system. The fact that vast amounts of student financial aid and other sources of funding have been made available to qualified persons is evidence of our dedication to this goal. This report examines the distribution of student financial aid in relation to women. Two significant factors must be remembered: (1) women comprise the majority of college and continuing education students today, and (2) public policy underlying financial aid gives little consideration to possible differences in the conditions affecting men's and women's need for aid. It is worth noting that in his recently published book, *Family and Nation* (1986), Senator Patrick Moynihan reports that the fastest growing poverty-stricken group in this country is children in a family headed by a single mother. Since a direct correlation can be drawn between earning power and educational attainment, it is clear where financial aid should be directed. Financial access to higher education for all students remains a noble yet elusive goal.

Although this report presents much hard data concerning student financial aid and women, it does not attempt to draw a causal relationship between inequities and women. Nevertheless, one cannot help but wonder whether inequities in the distribution and amount of aid would diminish or be eliminated if the financial aid policies were more attuned towards the needs of women. For example, the majority of part-time students are women, and under current policy part-time students have less opportunity to qualify for aid. More women than men are single heads-of-households, yet insufficient consideration is given toward child care expenses. Women continue to be paid less per hour than men, yet the maximum number of allowable work hours under scholarship programs are the same for women as for men. A rethinking of student aid policies could reduce some of the inequities.

To many people, these policies may seem to be primarily a state or federal issue. But since they directly affect the institution, faculty and administrators must work to influence the policy decisions regardless of where the locus of control originates. As the demographics of the student population continue to change, colleges and universities have a vested interest in insuring that all qualified students continue to have access to higher education.

Mary Moran, currently a program officer in the Office of Elementary and Secondary Education in the U.S. Department of Education, has compiled a definitive report on student financial aid and gender. Dr. Moran drew on her experience as a senior research associate for the National Commission on Student Financial Assistance, a Congressional commission that made policy recommendations for the reauthorization of Higher Education Act, and as an employee in the U.S. Department of Education to gain access to innumerable documents and studies, many of which are reproduced here in tabular form. This report will not only be read, but will be referred to time and again for its ready compilation of data.

The Association for the Study of Higher Education and the ERIC Clearinghouse on Higher Education would like to thank the Exxon Education Foundation for their generous grant in support of this project, which aided in the development of the manuscript and in providing wider distribution of this report.

**Jonathan D. Fife**
Series Editor
Professor and Director
ERIC Clearinghouse on Higher Education
The George Washington University

# ACKNOWLEDGMENTS

Much of the information in this report is based on research findings from the National Commission on Student Financial Assistance and on a review of data bases from other national sources. The National Commission investigated several congressionally determined policy questions, produced seven subcommittee reports, conducted over 20 public hearings around the country, and contracted for nearly 50 research studies. All recommendations, reports, and findings are available through the ERIC Document Reproduction Service or the ERIC microfiche collections, and all transcripts of meetings and public hearings are available from the National Archives. An initial paper, "Student Financial Assistance: Next Steps to Improving Education and Economic Opportunity for Women," which contains extensive tables on enrollment trends, participation rates for students, and average amounts of awards, is available through ERIC (ED 246 712).

Many individuals assisted in this project, and it would take several pages to acknowledge those who spent valuable time sharing information, producing computer printouts, debating the federal role in achieving equity, and reviewing drafts. I am particularly grateful to my friends and colleagues at the National Commission on Student Financial Assistance and the U.S. Department of Education. The views expressed are my own, however, and do not necessarily reflect those of the National Commission or the U.S. Department of Education.

Some people took risks and were particularly influential in the completion of this report. Virginia Hodgkinson recommended me for working at the National Commission. Rick Jerue, my former boss, was patient and supportive while I learned the ropes of student aid. Elaine El-Khawas prepared a policy brief for the American Council on Education. Senator Orrin Hatch pushed through a new mandate in the Education Amendments of 1984: that the National Advisory Council on Women's Education Programs include members who are "representative of and expert in student financial assistance programs." It is now law. (And, as this book goes to press, a few of the issues raised in the report are being given serious consideration in the final passage of the Higher Education Act.) Jon Fife, director of the ERIC Clearinghouse on Higher Education, was a pivotal person in making this publication a reality.

Chris Rigaux, publications coordinator for the Clearinghouse, and Barbara Fishel, my editor, provided invaluable assistance. David Gardner, president of the University of California and commission member for whom I worked as subcommittee senior research staff, inspired me to persist in what I believe is right. This report is made possible with funding from the Exxon Education Foundation, and I express my thanks to Dick Johnson of the Foundation.

# EMERGING ECONOMIC TRENDS IN POSTSECONDARY EDUCATION

Since 1970, the overall growth in college enrollments is attributed to the increased participation of women in higher education, reflecting new economic needs, changing social attitudes, and passage of civil rights laws. In fact, college enrollment of women increased 77.4 percent from 1970 to 1980, compared to a 22.6 percent increase for men. Indeed, women are contributing to an emerging new style of post-secondary education throughout the country but confront disproportionate financial burdens in paying for college.

Patterns of enrollment, economic characteristics, and needs related to financial aid differ for women and men, and student aid analysts and college officials would do well to learn those differences. While a vast amount of research has contributed to understanding educational equity for women, virtually no investigation has addressed the impact on women of policies on student aid and college costs, especially in such areas as ability to pay for college, choosing and attending a college, loan repayment, wage rates for college work, participation in student aid programs, and policies that are contradictory with public welfare programs.

*Between the academic years 1973–74 and 1982–83 alone, charges for undergraduate tuition, room, and board rose by 94 percent. . . .*

### College Costs and Enrollment Trends

While inflation is below 4 percent, the average price for 1985–86 tuitions jumped about 8 percent, the same rise as for the 1984–85 school year. The average cost for the school year (tuition and fees only) is $1,242 at public four-year schools, $5,418 at private four-year schools, $659 at public two-year schools, and $3,719 at private two-year schools (College Board 1985). These costs at least double when living expenses, books and supplies, personal expenses, and transportation are added. Between the academic years 1973–74 and 1982–83 alone, charges for undergraduate tuition, room, and board rose by 94 percent at public institutions and by 119 percent at private institutions (U.S. Department of Education 1984c). Such trends will result in many students' being unable to achieve their full educational potential.

At the same time, many complex variables enter into the process of selecting a college—parents' levels of education and expectations, academic ability and potential, influence by peers, and motivation—with the family's socioeconomic status predominant (Fife 1975; Litten, Sullivan, and

Brodigan 1983; Peterson and Rosco 1983) (see figure 1).
Yet increased college costs clearly have made the availability of and information about financial aid from whatever
source an increasingly important, many times pivotal, variable for attending college.

Female high school graduates' rates of participation in
postsecondary education have increased noticeably—from
53 percent in 1972 to 56 percent in 1980—and that increase
occurred in both four-year institutions (from 29 percent to
32 percent) and two-year institutions (from 15 percent to 19
percent) (U.S. Department of Education 1984c). The participation rates for high school graduates immediately following graduation, however, is 77 percent among students
of high socioeconomic status (82 percent for females, 73
percent for males) but only 35 percent among students of
low socioeconomic status (37 percent for females, 32 percent for males) (U.S. Department of Education 1984c).
And the dropout rate among females after they enter college is higher than that of males.

College costs are projected to continue to increase substantially as the result of high recurring costs associated
with tenured faculty, bargaining agreements, maintenance
of facilities, sharply higher insurance premiums, purchase
of computers, and intense lobbying pressure on Congress
to increase student aid, allowing institutions to increase
charges for tuition without raising the net cost for students.
While some argue that cost containment is not a serious
policy concern among postsecondary institutions or Washington lobbyists, charges for tuition and student aid now
constitute a significant and growing source of revenue in
university budgets.

Examining the economic issues underlying changing patterns of enrollment is necessary to understand the financial
needs of both men and women and to make the distribution
of student aid more equitable. Trends in college enrollment
since 1960 show that the participation of females is directly
related to costs: the higher the tuition and living costs, the
less likely women are to enroll. Women consequently
depend on low-cost institutions, outnumbering males in
undergraduate public four-year and two-year colleges,
while males outnumber females in high-cost private institutions (see table 1). Thus, low tuition in land-grant colleges,
state colleges and universities, and community colleges has

# FIGURE 1
## THE COLLEGE SELECTION PROCESS

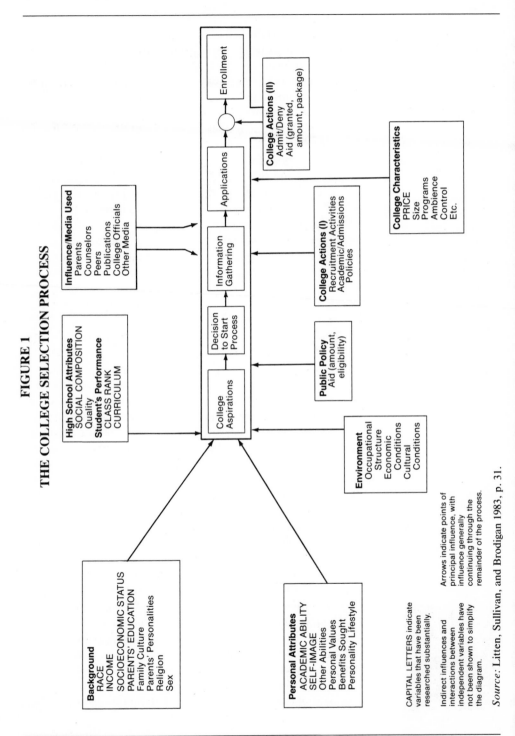

**Background**
RACE
INCOME
SOCIOECONOMIC STATUS
PARENTS' EDUCATION
Family Culture
Parents' Personalities
Religion
Sex

**Personal Attributes**
ACADEMIC ABILITY
SELF-IMAGE
Other Abilities
Personal Values
Benefits Sought
Personality Lifestyle

**High School Attributes**
SOCIAL COMPOSITION
Quality
**Student's Performance**
CLASS RANK
CURRICULUM

**Influence/Media Used**
Parents
Counselors
Peers
Publications
College Officials
Other Media

**Environment**
Occupational
Structure
Economic
Conditions
Cultural
Conditions

**Public Policy**
Aid (amount,
eligibility)

**College Actions (I)**
Recruitment Activities
Academic/Admissions
Policies

**College Characteristics**
PRICE
Size
Programs
Ambience
Control
Etc.

**College Actions (II)**
Admit/Deny
Aid (granted,
amount, package)

College Aspirations
Decision to Start Process
Information Gathering
Applications
Enrollment

CAPITAL LETTERS indicate
variables that have been
researched substantially.

Indirect influences and
interactions between
independent variables have
not been shown to simplify
the diagram.

Arrows indicate points of
principal influence, with
influence generally
continuing through the
remainder of the process.

*Source:* Litten, Sullivan, and Brodigan 1983, p. 31.

TABLE 1

## SIGNIFICANT ENROLLMENT TRENDS

|  | Fall 1979 | Fall 1980 | Fall 1981 | Fall 1982 |
|---|---|---|---|---|
| **Public, Total** | 9,036,822 | 9,457,394 | 9,647,032 | 9,696,087 |
| Men | 4,368,979 | 4,522,587 | 4,586,800 | 4,632,888 |
| Women | 4,667,843 | 4,934,807 | 5,060,232 | 5,063,199 |
| | | | | |
| **Public Two-Year** | 4,065,627 | 4,283,678 | 4,432,157 | 4,463,945 |
| Men | 1,862,360 | 1,926,270 | 1,977,758 | 1,998,341 |
| Women | 2,203,267 | 2,357,408 | 2,454,399 | 2,465,604 |
| | | | | |
| **Private, Total** | 2,533,077 | 2,639,501 | 2,724,640 | 2,729,693 |
| Men | 1,313,898 | 1,351,787 | 1,388,256 | 1,398,496 |
| Women | 1,219,179 | 1,287,714 | 1,336,384 | 1,331,197 |
| | | | | |
| **Specialized Pro-prietary** | | | | |
| Total | 13,545 | 18,290 | 21,106 | 22,666 |
| Men | 10,550 | 13,302 | 15,541 | 17,299 |
| Women | 2,995 | 4,988 | 5,565 | 5,367 |

*Source:* U.S. Department of Education 1984d. (See also table A-3 in Appendix A.)

become one of the best mechanisms for achieving educational opportunity (American Association of State Colleges and Universities 1974; Johnson and Smith 1984).

A few exceptions defy the national statistics. The elite women's colleges—Barnard, Sarah Lawrence, Mount Holyoke, Wellesley, Vassar, Radcliffe—continually have the highest costs of all colleges, now averaging up to $16,000 per school year, yet receive among the highest contributions from alumnae, lessening the burden on women somewhat. Other expensive institutions with notable female enrollments—American University, St. Louis University, New York University, Loyola University, Southern Methodist University—are nationally recognized for aggressive recruiting, special services and scholarship programs for women, notable numbers of women in leadership positions, and explicit policies for ensuring fairness to women (Howe, Howard, and Strauss 1982).

Significant increases in enrollment of females have also coincided with the expansion of federal legislation and poli-

cies aimed at reducing barriers to higher education for women. In particular, Title IX of the Education Amendments of 1972, explicitly prohibiting discrimination in admissions, athletics, and student activities, has had a salutary effect. As a result of Title IX assurances' being a precondition to receiving federal funds, many institutions have improved their practices and eliminated discriminatory barriers, and some believe that Title IX has contributed more to the increase in female enrollments than has the availability of student aid.

Consequently, increased enrollment of women has been most significant in low-cost two-year public institutions, where females outnumber males nearly two to one. The expansion of community colleges offering open admissions, low tuition, and flexible schedules enables many women to combine work, family responsibilities, and education. Enrollments of black and other minority females have risen somewhat in low-cost community colleges and historically black colleges (Fleming, Payne, and Kirschner 1984; Hill 1983). Such increases also reflect higher aspirations among female high school graduates as well as changes in how both sexes view women (Astin 1982). Recent research warns, however, that as college costs increase and student aid decreases, the very institutions with high female enrollments are not meeting enrollment targets (Andersen, 1986), suggesting that women are perhaps being priced out of postsecondary education.

Significant differences exist in enrollment trends between genders by age category (see table 2), yet despite impressive rates of increases, there is cause for concern about the economic needs of women. Actual enrollments of females are highest in career areas having the lowest potential salaries. The fastest-growing and highest-cost career areas—computer sciences and engineering, medicine and law—have the lowest female enrollments. In 1982, women earned 50.3 percent of the bachelor's degrees granted (75 percent in education, 6 percent in computer sciences), 50.8 percent of the master's degrees (72 percent in education, 9 percent in computer sciences), and 32.1 percent of the doctorates (49 percent in education, 5 percent in computer sciences). And although the ratio of female seniors expecting to attend graduate or professional school more than doubled from 1972 to 1983, postsecond-

## TABLE 2

### ENROLLMENT TRENDS BY AGE CATEGORY AND SEX: 1970–1982

| Males | Percent Increase |
|---|---|
| Ages 16–24 | 19 |
| Ages 25–34 | 35 |
| Ages 35 & over | 64 |
| | |
| **Females** | |
| Ages 16–24 | 38 |
| Ages 25–34 | 72 |
| Ages 35 & over | 80 |

*Source:* National Association of Student Financial Aid Administrators 1985a, p. 3.

ary dropout rates are higher for women, particularly among independent and graduate women students.

Furthermore, the figures in table 2 hide the fact that women frequently incur greater college costs than males as a consequence of receiving less student aid and are more likely to be independent, part-time, adult, and unclassified students. Women take longer to complete a degree and are more likely to enroll as transfer students, hold financial responsibilities for child care, and be required to take remedial courses in math and science (American College Testing 1976 to 1980; Cross and McCartan 1984; Fenske, Hearn, and Curry 1985).

Of the 1.7 million adults participating in education (all as part-time students) whose annual incomes are under $7,500, 69 percent are women. For those whose annual incomes range from $7,500 to $14,999, 64 percent are female, while for annual incomes at or above $25,000, the proportion of male and female participants is virtually equal (U.S. Department of Education 1984c). In comparing 1974 and 1981, the National Commission on Student Financial Assistance found that participation rates for dependent women exceeded those for dependent men, except in the lowest income category (under $6,000 annually). Although participation rates for women have increased overall, the rate actually declined among dependent students between 1974 and 1981 in the lowest income group, while it increased for almost all other categories of income. Thus, students with the greatest financial need and the lowest participation rates showed the greatest decline in enrollments (Lee 1983).

## Transition from High School

High school dropout rates, while primarily associated with low socioeconomic status, also show significant differences between genders that student aid analysts need to be concerned about. Females drop out of high school mainly because of family-related reasons, while males drop out because of school-related issues—they dislike school or their grades are poor (U.S. Department of Education 1984c). The most significant cause is pregnancy, accounting for 23 percent of female sophomore dropouts. Teenage mothers tend not to return to school, do not receive information about student aid, and generally become early recipients of public welfare. Of particular concern are high school reentry rates as they relate to test scores. "The contrast between males and females [is] particularly striking. Compared to the low test quartile (8 percent), five times as many males in the high test quartile (40 percent) [reenter] high school, whereas for women, the rate [is] merely doubled (9 percent compared to 18 percent)" (U.S. Department of Education 1984c, p. 219).

## The Effect of Education on Potential Earnings

Increasing the economic capacity of individuals and of the nation has been an important rationale for justifying student financial assistance. Student aid clearly plays an important role in creating greater educational expectations and a national policy encouraging college attendance (Jerue 1983; Miller 1984). Although the value and worth of higher education are occasionally challenged, actual statistics on poverty rates, hourly wages, and lifetime earnings indicate that some type of postsecondary education pays off—and more so for women (see table 3).

In fact, "getting a good job" is a significantly greater reason for choosing a particular college for women than for men. And as more women move into positions previously held exclusively by men, academic credentials and attending selective colleges may actually become more important (Rosenfeld and Hearn 1982). The greater an individual's

## TABLE 3

## MEDIAN INCOME OF YEAR-ROUND FULL-TIME WORKERS, BY EDUCATIONAL ATTAINMENT AND SEX: 1981[a]

| Years of School Completed | Median Income | | Income Gap in Dollars | Women's Income as a Percent of Men's | Percent Men's Income Exceeded Women's | Marginal Dollar Value of Increased Educational Attainment | |
|---|---|---|---|---|---|---|---|
| | Women | Men | | | | Women | Men |
| **Elementary School** | | | | | | | |
| Less than 8 years | $ 8,419 | $12,866 | $ 4,447 | 65.4 | 52.8 | – | – |
| 8 years | 9,723 | 16,084 | 6,361 | 60.5 | 65.4 | $1,304 | $3,218 |
| **High School** | | | | | | | |
| 1 to 3 years | 10,043 | 16,938 | 6,895 | 59.3 | 68.7 | 320 | 854 |
| 4 years | 12,332 | 20,598 | 8,266 | 59.9 | 67.0 | 2,289 | 3,660 |
| **College** | | | | | | | |
| 1 to 3 years | 14,343 | 22,565 | 8,222 | 63.6 | 57.3 | 2,011 | 1,967 |
| 4 years | 16,322 | 26,394 | 10,072 | 61.8 | 61.7 | 1,979 | 3,829 |
| 5 years or more | 20,148 | 30,434 | 10,286 | 66.2 | 51.1 | 3,826 | 4,040 |

[a]Persons 25 years of age and over.

*Source:* U.S. Department of Labor 1984, p. 36.

educational attainment, the greater the potential employment and earnings, particularly for women. As table 3 notes, however, within every educational level and age group, young women earn less per hour than comparable young men (Kolstad 1982; Tierney 1982; U.S. Department of Labor 1984). "More than half of all women with four years of college had incomes in 1981 that were only slightly higher than the median income for men who had . . . completed [only] the eighth grade. Women with four years of high school but no college had a lower median income than did men who had not completed elementary school" (U.S. Department of Labor 1984, p. 98).

*Women with four years of high school but no college had a lower median income than did men who had not completed elementary school.*

More recently, the value of a college degree has even been at issue in divorce cases. Judges have ruled that a woman is entitled to a portion of a husband's income when she has delayed an education herself and worked to make sure her husband has completed school, particularly in the areas of medicine and law. And more states are considering legislation that requires judges to consider the financial contributions of each spouse to the education of the other when their property is divided in divorce proceedings. More often than not, the spouse who sacrifices and works for the benefit of the other, enhancing that person's earning capacity, is the wife.

Furthermore, statistics show significant relationships between educational level attained and poverty rates (see table A-11 in Appendix A). Two out of every three adults living in poverty are women. And even though poverty rates decrease with additional years of education, poverty rates for women with one or more years of college are substantially higher than for similar males (U.S. Department of Education 1984c).

### Significant Trends in Student Aid

Over 80 percent of student financial assistance comes from the federal government in the form of loans, grants, and work study programs that are made available directly through postsecondary institutions and indirectly by subsidizing interest and/or guaranteeing loans through state guarantee agencies, lending institutions, and institutions of higher education (College Board 1985). This portion amounts to over half of the total budget for the U.S. Department of Education, or more than $10 billion for fiscal year 1986. The remaining aid is generated by state programs, institutional sources, private initiatives, and corporate benefits that pay tuition. Over $21 billion is now available from both government and private sources.

Nevertheless, noticeable differences between genders and problems occur in student aid programs. One analysis (see table 4) of all student aid obtained by low-income undergraduates for the 1981–82 academic year reveals that for every dollar a man receives, a woman receives 68 cents in college earnings, 73 cents in grants, and 84 cents in loans (U.S. Department of Education 1983).

Considerable gaps between genders appear in self-help programs, and that gap is greater for part-time than for full-time students (Leslie 1982). Women are less able than men to depend on earnings, savings, and loans for college costs; as a consequence, they tend to receive larger amounts of aid from family or friends out of necessity. They receive fewer dollars in self-help, grants, work, and scholarships (Davis 1977; U.S. Department of Education 1983). The more significant differences appear in discretionary programs such as college work, merit scholarships, research assistantships, and corporate benefits that pay tuition.

These trends raise questions about the appropriate balance and suitability of student aid policies. The following sections describe in more detail issues of gender in student aid policy, review the patterns of distribution of student aid, and suggest actions for improving women's receipt of student aid and thus their economic status.

## TABLE 4

### DIFFERENCES IN TOTAL AVERAGE GRANTS, LOANS, AND EARNINGS, BY TYPE OF INSTITUTION AND SEX: 1980–81 AND 1981–82[a]

| | Total Grant Amounts[b] | | Total Loan Amounts[b] | | Total Earnings[b] | |
|---|---|---|---|---|---|---|
| | 1980–81 | 1981–82 | 1980–81 | 1981–82 | 1980–81 | 1981–82 |
| **Public Two-Year** | | | | | | |
| Male | $1,142 | $1,362 | $ 754 | $1,408 | $ 711 | $ 764 |
| Female | 1,016 | 947 | 824 | 1,398 | 540 | 522 |
| **Public Four-Year** | | | | | | |
| Male | 1,900 | 2,034 | 1,329 | 1,528 | 1,007 | 1,237 |
| Female | 1,575 | 1,448 | 860 | 1,220 | 681 | 790 |
| **Private Four-Year** | | | | | | |
| Male | 3,323 | 3,613 | 1,871 | 2,228 | 884 | 1,158 |
| Female | 3,022 | 3,081 | 1,352 | 1,871 | 671 | 927 |
| **Vocational**[c] | | | | | | |
| Male | 1,303 | 1,481 | 2,137 | 1,901 | 812 | 534 |
| Female | 1,260 | 1,025 | 1,362 | 1,976 | 848 | 481 |
| **All Institutions** | | | | | | |
| Male | 1,950 | 2,218 | 1,557 | 1,766 | 873 | 1,014 |
| Female | 1,688 | 1,609 | 1,152 | 1,492 | 650 | 694 |

[a]The base for average dollar amounts is all low-income (less than $12,000 annually) 1980 high school seniors enrolled in postsecondary education in 1980–81 and 1981–82.

[b]Average amount per individual.

[c]Includes all vocational and technical institutions as well as proprietary institutions.

*Source:* U.S. Department of Education 1983.

# ISSUES OF GENDER IN STUDENT AID POLICY

Disproportionate financial burdens confront women attending postsecondary institutions, among them low salaries while paying back Guaranteed Student Loans, lack of recognition for academic merit, few opportunities for graduate research assistantships, lack of allowances for child care in establishing costs of attendance, barriers to employers' benefit programs that pay tuition, contradictory policies between public welfare and student aid programs, and biased assumptions in needs analysis systems. By examining the impact on men versus women of their student aid policy, college officials can adapt and restructure programs and practices. Given the importance of equal opportunity in achieving educational excellence, the underlying causes of inequity must be sought and corrected. Although effects are easier to determine than causes, the following discussion describes current problems and suggests possible solutions, recognizing that further research is necessary to clarify causes.

## Loan Burden, Default, and Bankruptcy

Inadequate data and formulas for calculating and reporting default rates for student loans can conceal problems and exaggerate improvements (Lyke 1976), which occurs in determining impact of student loan burdens, defaults, and bankruptcies on women. A critical dilemma facing student loan officials is the question of how to curb rising defaults while at the same time ensuring students' access to postsecondary education. Yet variables identified by a U.S. Department of Education study to be strong predictors of defaulting on a loan—withdrawing from school, being black, having a low income and holding a relatively larger loan, being an independent student at the time of taking the loan, and being divorced or separated with a low family income (Kuch 1978)—are not monitored in final reports for Guaranteed Student Loans (GSLs) or National Direct Student Loans (NDSLs). None of the state guarantee agencies collect information about gender for defaults on GSLs, nor is information about gender available for other major loan programs—Health Education Assistance Loans (HEALs), Health Profession Student Loans (HPSLs), Nursing Student Loans (NSLs), or the Parent Loans for Undergraduate Students (PLUS) program. Further, in the most recent and extensive research by the National Commission on

Student Financial Assistance on students' rates of defaulting on loans, any data describing the sex, race, or income of defaulters was not studied because it was not available (Lee 1983).

Substantial evidence indicates that women experience significant financial burdens while trying to pay back student loans and thus are more prone to default and to declare bankruptcy. Women who rely heavily on loans are more likely to withdraw from school, while women who receive outright grants are more likely than other women aid recipients to persist (Astin 1975). The National Association of Student Financial Aid Administrators warns that "women report greater needs to work two or more jobs to handle loan repayments" (Boyd and Martin 1986, p. 17), a burden that results from low earnings, the tendency to major in fields known for low salaries, the disproportionate effect of layoffs on women, and the greater likelihood of being independent students or attending proprietary institutions with the highest default rates. And a woman's being black (or other minority) or assuming her husband's debt if she is married increases the burden. Furthermore, pregnancy is not an allowable justification for receiving a disability deferment.

> *Concern about levels of indebtedness must be conditioned on the basis of the student's anticipated income upon graduation. . . . It is apparent that undergraduate students in the occupations traditionally held by women (nursing, teaching, social work), which are characterized by very low starting salaries, will feel the greatest impact of education loans on their posteducation ability and willingness to borrow* (Johnson 1983, p. 18).

An extensive study of commercial bankruptcies by the Brookings Institution concluded that divorced women tend to be three times as likely as divorced men to declare bankruptcy (17 percent versus 6 percent), and of the 2 percent bankrupt individuals who were widowed, *all* were women (Stanley and Girth 1971, p. 42). Furthermore, bankruptcies increase during periods of high unemployment and national recession. Several characteristics tend to trigger bankruptcies and adversely affect women more than men:

1. Those with low-paying jobs have the highest tendency to declare bankruptcy.

2. The earnings of a woman upon a divorce tend to be substantially less than her husband's, if she has any earnings at all.
3. Bearing and raising children become an added expense as well as an obstacle to the mother's gainful employment (Cowans 1975, p. 302).

A further consideration, highlighted during public hearings of the National Commission on Student Financial Assistance, may be the form of assistance offered:

*There may be students who are unwilling to borrow because they are in a field of study where the level of compensation is very modest indeed compared with those studying in some other field, and so they wouldn't even show up on the guaranteed student loan program at all much less the default rate. . . . If the default rate for the students in the field where the prospect of earnings is not very bright is higher than in fields where the prospect for earnings is higher, then that perhaps ought to offer us some guidance in respect to how we undertake to provide student financial assistance in respect to whether it should be work study or guaranteed student loans* (Gardner 1983, p. 144).

Meanwhile, curtailing the increases in rates of default on student loans and the expenses of collecting debts is now a necessary federal priority: Federal costs to pay off defaulted loans have surpassed $5 billion (U.S. Department of Education 1986). As a result of the Debt Collection Act of 1982 authorizing the reporting of delinquent borrowers to credit bureaus, the U.S. Department of Education now works with four nationwide credit bureaus to aid in the collection of outstanding debts (Dexter 1984). As defaults have increased, the profit margins of collection agencies have also increased significantly. In 1984 alone, over $2.4 billion was identified as delinquent loans; approximately $30 billion in college loans was outstanding in 1985. More recently, implementation of the Federal Income Tax Refund Offset Program resulted in the recovery of over $116 million in early 1986.

Compounding the problem, dependency on loans has risen as college costs increase and sources of scholarships decline (Hechinger 1986). The average indebtedness for undergraduates, adjusting for inflation, soared from $2,100 in 1975 to $7,900 in 1984. For graduate students, debts averaging $15,000 to $20,000 are not uncommon. (Other issues specific to GSLs and NDSLs are discussed in the next section.) Evidence suggests that examining defaulters' characteristics, including gender, and adjusting student aid programs to ensure access to students found most likely to default might curtail the rising federal costs of defaults and the personal agony of being in default or bankruptcy (Davis 1985; Hauptman 1976).

**Merit Scholarships**
In the current climate of improving educational excellence, increasing competition for a declining pool of students, and decreasing federal support for student aid based on need, institutions of higher education have intensified their efforts to recruit students by offering lucrative grants and scholarships based on merit (Hechinger 1986; Van Dusen and Higginbotham 1984). Yet evidence shows that females with high academic achievements receive fewer and smaller awards than their male counterparts. The award of merit-based scholarships is highly discretionary and thus more subject to biases based on gender. A significant trend of concern to women is that at public institutions in 1984–85 the number of recipients of state work/study programs based on need declined by 39,670, while the number of state non-need-based "merit" grants increased by 39,311 recipients (Stampen 1985).

One of the most prestigious awards for academic excellence is the National Merit Scholarship; its receipt virtually guarantees access to any postsecondary institution in the country. In 1985, 2,280 females and 3,741 males were merit scholars. The most significant disparities occur in math, science, and engineering; for example, 48 females and 317 males won in electrical engineering, 56 females and 265 males in physics, and 49 females and 264 males in computer sciences (National Merit Scholarship Corporation 1986, p. 8). Even worse, the number of female recipients has decreased notably since 1984, while the overall total of merit scholarships awarded has increased. The proportion of females in 1984 was 40.2 percent (out of 5,858 total awards); the proportion of females in 1985 was 37.9 percent (out of 6,021 awards) (National Merit Scholarship Corporation 1985, 1986).

Potential barriers may exist in nominating, screening, and selecting recipients, as evidenced by the fact that women's receipt of merit scholarships does not reflect enrollment rates. Recipients are selected by a committee comprised of college admissions officers and secondary school counselors, and the attitudes and biases of those on the committee play a role in the selection of recipients.

Another prestigious merit award is the Rhodes Scholarship, which only in the last few years has been awarded to women. Prospective Rhodes Scholars are first identified by selection committees throughout the country. Each state committee may nominate two candidates for consideration by a district committee, which in turn may designate four candidates from the group of 12 to 14 district finalists as Rhodes Scholars–elect (Rhodes Scholarship Trust 1983, p. 9). Clearly, the recognition of women for outstanding scholastic achievement depends upon the attitudes and sensitivity of individuals holding the power to award financial resources. And women themselves tend not to have authority in the final selection of scholars, which may be another reason for the poor showing of women recognized for academic performance.

Further, the award of merit scholarships on the basis of achievement and performance on aptitude tests like ACT and SAT favors males over females, especially in math and sciences. Besides being used extensively in college admissions, these tests, when used as well for determining scholarships, are significant factors in deterring women from careers in math, computer sciences, and the physical sciences. By the end of high school, significant differences occur between males and females in math and science ACT and SAT scores (see table 5 and table A-12 in Appendix A) (Educational Testing Service 1984; Gordon and Addison 1985). Although women receive higher grades in school, their average score is 59 points lower than men's on the SAT. The trend is similar for the Graduate Record Exam quantitative test, in which males are four times as likely to score above 700 (Klitgaard 1985, p. 160). Thus, for highly competitive scholarships where scores on such tests determine the applicants, women are being shortchanged and weeded out because the tests underestimate their ability to

*Although women receive higher grades in school, their average score is 59 points lower than men's on the SAT.*

## TABLE 5
## SAT SCORE AVERAGES FOR COLLEGE-BOUND SENIORS

|      | Verbal | | | Math | | |
|------|-------|---------|-------|-------|---------|-------|
|      | Males | Females | Total | Males | Females | Total |
| **1980** | 428 | 420 | 424 | 491 | 443 | 466 |
| **1981** | 430 | 418 | 424 | 492 | 443 | 466 |
| **1982** | 431 | 421 | 426 | 493 | 443 | 467 |
| **1983** | 430 | 420 | 425 | 493 | 445 | 468 |
| **1984** | 433 | 420 | 426 | 495 | 449 | 471 |
| **1985** | 437 | 425 | 431 | 499 | 452 | 475 |
| **1986** | 437 | 426 | 431 | 501 | 451 | 475 |

*Source:* College Entrance Examination Board 1980 to 1986.

succeed. Adding to the dilemma—and the cost—is that women are enrolling in coaching courses in increasing numbers. Two-thirds of the students at the popular Princeton Review coaching school (which boasts an average improvement of 150 points but costs $495 a course) in 1985 were women.

The gender gap in quantitative test performance, although narrowing, is more a consequence of differences in the pattern of quantitative coursework taken by males and females in high school than of any differences in inherent intelligence. And at least one study found that increasing females' participation in high school advanced math and science courses to equal at least males' participation would reduce differences between genders in quantitative test scores (Pallas and Alexander 1983).

On the other hand, women are still recognized more for beauty than for intelligence, and more women are entering Miss America pageants each year, partly because of increasing scholarship awards. The Miss America Scholarship Corporation, the largest scholarship foundation for women in the world, gives out close to $5 million each year, and much credit is due the corporation for emphasizing intellectual achievement and potential as criteria for winning in local, state, and national pageants and for substantially increasing scholarship awards (Miller 1985).

### Independent Students
Independent students—displaced homemakers, women returning to college, single parents, and migrant women—

are of particular concern to policy makers. Homemakers facing the sudden death of a spouse or divorce are especially vulnerable to economic undertows: Many times they have no job skills or have not finished school. Men's standard of living upon divorce, for example, rises 72 percent in the first year after divorce, while women's and children's drops 42 percent (Weitzman 1985). A significant social development of recent times is the swift rise of one-parent families, now accounting for 26 percent of all families with children under 18, with nine-tenths headed by women who are disproportionately black and poor. While the latest national poverty rate is 15.2 percent, it is 40 percent for single-parent families headed by white women, 60 percent for those headed by black women, and 70 percent for those headed by Hispanic women (Rich 1985).

In fact, single women with children have the most critical unmet financial need under current student aid policies. Not only do independent female students average lower tuitions and higher total costs of attendance than independent male students; independent students with children are more than twice as likely to be female (see table 6) and are nearly five times as likely to be older than 24 years of age. About 60 percent of all such students are enrolled part time in community colleges (Fenske, Hearn, and Curry 1985; Stampen 1985).

Women are twice as likely as men to be classified as independent students at the freshman level (66 percent versus 34 percent) (American College Testing 1980) and have more than twice the unmet need of dependent students. While the number of independent females is twice that of independent males at the freshman level, the proportion of independent females to independent males at the graduate level is dramatically reversed (45 percent versus 55 percent) (see table 7). This drop is particularly pronounced between the senior level and the graduate level, suggesting that women are not able to cope with significant amounts of unmet financial need.

As a consequence of having great unmet financial need and having to cover a larger proportion of college costs, women tend to drop out of school, enroll part time, increase their work load, or assume more loans (American Association of State Colleges and Universities 1974; Dunkle 1980; Johnson 1983; National Urban League 1984).

# TABLE 6
## DISTRIBUTION OF UNMET NEED BY STATUS OF DEPENDENCY AND SEX: 1982–83 AND 1983–84

| | Dependent | | Independent with Children | | Independent without Children | |
|---|---|---|---|---|---|---|
| | No. of Students | Average Need per Recipient | No. of Students | Average Need per Recipient | No. of Students | Average Need per Recipient |
| **1982–83** | | | | | | |
| Male | 4,524 | $2,126 | 937 | $4,005 | 3,289 | $2,114 |
| Female | 4,927 | 2,090 | 2,158 | 4,168 | 2,648 | 2,215 |
| **1983–84** | | | | | | |
| Male | 5,091 | 2,170 | 1,039 | 4,540 | 3,788 | 2,308 |
| Female | 5,645 | 2,112 | 2,293 | 4,163 | 2,909 | 2,357 |

Source: Fenske, Hearn, and Curry 1985, p. 14.

TABLE 7

PERCENTAGE OF STUDENT AID APPLICANTS WITH NEED ACCORDING TO CLASS LEVEL, BY SEX: 1974–75 TO 1979–80[a]

| | 1974–75 | | | 1975–76 | | | 1976–77 | | | 1977–78 | | | 1978–79 | | | 1979–80 | | |
|---|---|---|---|---|---|---|---|---|---|---|---|---|---|---|---|---|---|---|
| | M | F | T | M | F | T | M | F | T | M | F | T | M | F | T | M | F | T |
| **Dependent** | (N = 19,474) | | | (N = 27,892) | | | (N = 30,333) | | | (N = 23,580) | | | (N = 33,140) | | | (N = 35,424) | | |
| Freshman | 45 | 55 | 47 | 47 | 53 | 49 | 45 | 55 | 38 | 45 | 55 | 35 | 45 | 55 | 44 | 46 | 54 | 42 |
| Sophomore | 44 | 56 | 23 | 43 | 57 | 21 | 43 | 57 | 22 | 42 | 58 | 22 | 44 | 56 | 24 | 44 | 56 | 23 |
| Junior | 44 | 56 | 16 | 45 | 55 | 15 | 45 | 55 | 14 | 43 | 57 | 15 | 44 | 55 | 16 | 44 | 56 | 16 |
| Senior | 47 | 53 | 9 | 43 | 57 | 9 | 46 | 54 | 9 | 43 | 57 | 10 | 44 | 56 | 12 | 47 | 53 | 11 |
| Graduate student | 58 | 42 | 3 | 59 | 41 | 3 | 53 | 47 | 2 | 57 | 43 | 3 | 55 | 45 | 2 | 58 | 42 | 1 |
| Other or unknown | 44 | 56 | 2 | 43 | 57 | 2 | 49 | 51 | 15 | 49 | 51 | 15 | 47 | 53 | 1 | 47 | 53 | 7 |
| Totals | 45 | 55 | 100 | 46 | 54 | 100 | 46 | 54 | 100 | 45 | 55 | 100 | 45 | 55 | 100 | 46 | 54 | 100 |
| **Self-Supporting** | (N = 5,533) | | | (N = 7,419) | | | (N = 9,343) | | | (N = 7,803) | | | (N = 10,133) | | | (N = 11,214) | | |
| Freshman | 38 | 62 | 24 | 39 | 61 | 26 | 38 | 62 | 23 | 36 | 64 | 19 | 32 | 68 | 22 | 34 | 66 | 22 |
| Sophomore | 44 | 56 | 22 | 39 | 61 | 22 | 44 | 56 | 22 | 40 | 60 | 21 | 38 | 62 | 21 | 37 | 63 | 20 |
| Junior | 49 | 51 | 21 | 48 | 52 | 19 | 49 | 51 | 18 | 48 | 52 | 19 | 45 | 55 | 22 | 43 | 57 | 21 |
| Senior | 52 | 48 | 15 | 54 | 46 | 14 | 53 | 47 | 15 | 53 | 47 | 17 | 50 | 50 | 20 | 49 | 51 | 21 |
| Graduate student | 62 | 38 | 15 | 60 | 40 | 14 | 56 | 44 | 12 | 56 | 44 | 16 | 55 | 45 | 12 | 55 | 45 | 11 |
| Other or unknown | 40 | 60 | 4 | 35 | 65 | 4 | 41 | 59 | 9 | 39 | 61 | 7 | 40 | 60 | 3 | 35 | 65 | 6 |
| Totals | 47 | 53 | 100 | 46 | 54 | 100 | 46 | 54 | 100 | 45 | 55 | 100 | 43 | 57 | 100 | 42 | 58 | 100 |
| **All Applicants** | (N = 25,007) | | | (N = 35,311) | | | (N = 39,676) | | | (N = 31,383) | | | (N = 43,273) | | | (N = 46,638) | | |
| Freshman | 44 | 56 | 42 | 46 | 54 | 45 | 44 | 56 | 34 | 44 | 56 | 31 | 43 | 57 | 39 | 45 | 55 | 37 |
| Sophomore | 44 | 56 | 23 | 42 | 58 | 21 | 43 | 57 | 22 | 42 | 58 | 22 | 43 | 57 | 23 | 42 | 58 | 22 |
| Junior | 45 | 55 | 17 | 46 | 54 | 16 | 46 | 54 | 15 | 44 | 56 | 16 | 44 | 56 | 18 | 44 | 56 | 17 |
| Senior | 49 | 51 | 11 | 47 | 53 | 10 | 48 | 52 | 10 | 46 | 54 | 12 | 46 | 54 | 14 | 48 | 52 | 13 |
| Graduate student | 61 | 39 | 5 | 59 | 41 | 5 | 55 | 45 | 5 | 56 | 44 | 6 | 55 | 44 | 4 | 56 | 44 | 4 |
| Other or unknown | 42 | 58 | 2 | 40 | 60 | 3 | 48 | 52 | 14 | 47 | 53 | 13 | 44 | 56 | 2 | 45 | 55 | 7 |
| Totals | 45 | 55 | 100 | 46 | 54 | 100 | 46 | 54 | 100 | 45 | 55 | 100 | 44 | 56 | 100 | 45 | 55 | 100 |

[a]Based on all applicants with need.

Source: American College Testing 1974 to 1980.

Independent students attending private schools need an average of $1,447, while dependent students need an average of $247; independent students attending public schools need an average of $1,488, while dependent students fall $433 short; and independent students attending proprietary schools need an average of $2,160, while dependent students need $1,651 on average (El-Khawas 1983). During 1981–82, 13 percent of independent students attending college were in private schools, 39 percent were in public schools, and 54 percent were in proprietary schools (see tables A-8 and A-9 in Appendix A). Apparently, women facing great unmet need simply drop out.

### Part-time Students

Women far outnumber men as part-time students, both in numbers of enrollments and in rates of increase (see table 8). For example, female students 35 years and over outnumber males nearly 2 to 1 (13.5 percent to 7.5 percent), while most student aid programs restrict the participation of those students (U.S. Department of Commerce 1981).

Many women are prevented from taking more than one course because they have insufficient funds, responsibilities at work, or family commitments, or because they lack self-confidence (Dunkle 1980). Enrolling part time is becoming a major response to increased tuition. For many women, even the "half-time" threshold for federal aid is an obstacle. One analysis—of part-time students' use of financial aid in the state of New York—reports that *fewer than one out of every four* part-time undergraduate students receives some form of financial aid. The majority (67 percent) of this aid is from self-help programs, with GSLs alone accounting for 65 percent of all aid received. And the use and average award received by part-time students vary significantly by type of institution. Part-time graduate students receive the lowest number of awards of any category of students, with only one of every five students receiving some form of financial aid (Olinsky 1983, pp. 13–14). Further, virtually no institution—under 1 percent—uses the full 10 percent allowable for part-time students from campus-based allocations for student aid (College Work Study, Supplemental Educational Opportunity Grants, and National Direct Student Loans) (Davis 1983).

## TABLE 8

### COMPOSITION OF THE INCREASE IN ENROLLMENTS, BY SEX, ENROLLMENT STATUS, AND TYPE OF INSTITUTION: 1970–1980

|  | Percent of Increase | | Number of Increase |
|---|---|---|---|
| **Women** | | | |
| Full-time/Four-year | 23.6% | | 652,000 |
| Part-time/Two-year | 17.1 | | 474,000 |
| Full-time/Two-year | 11.1 | | 307,000 |
| Part-time/Four-year | 10.7 | | 298,000 |
|  | | 62.5% | |
| Full-time/Graduate | 7.6 | | 209,000 |
| Part-time/Graduate | 7.3 | | 202,000 |
|  | | 14.9% | |
| Total | | 77.4% | |
| **Men** | | | |
| Part-time/Two-year | 6.5% | | 181,000 |
| Part-time/Four-year | 5.7 | | 157,000 |
| Full-time/Four-year | 4.8 | | 134,000 |
| Part-time/Graduate | 2.6 | | 72,000 |
| Full-time/Graduate | 2.5 | | 68,000 |
| Full-time/Two-year | 0.5 | | 13,000 |
| Total | | 22.6% | |
| **Total** | | 100.0% | |

*Source:* U.S. Department of Commerce, Bureau of the Census 1981.

Institutions generally receive state funding on the basis of their full-time equivalent (FTE) enrollments; therefore, most university policies emphasize services to full-time students and part-time students depend more on their own resources.

*Part-time students receive very little in BEOG or any other grant aid, with other scholarships providing the major sources of grant support overall. . . . [And] loan amounts for the various loan programs are small. In comparison to full-time students, part-time students begin college by financing roughly half as large a share of total expenses from scholarships and grants, and this share gradually decreases. Essentially the same pattern prevails in the case of loans. Clearly, part-time students are much more on their own financially than are full-time students* (Leslie 1982, p. 60).

### Contradictory Policies in Public Welfare and Student Aid Programs

Compounding the economic hardships created by the labor market, women are placed at a further disadvantage by job histories that are generally not as extensive as those of men. When men are unemployed, they are more likely to receive unemployment compensation, disability payments, or workmen's compensation. Women, however, frequently do not qualify for such programs and must rely on public assistance. Conflicting purposes and procedures of public assistance programs result in disincentives for economically disadvantaged individuals who seek self-sufficiency through education. And these disincentives create barriers to college enrollment by reducing or categorically eliminating benefits for enrollment in college (Rosen 1983).

Individuals eligible for benefits from public assistance programs—three-fourths of whom are women—generally are required to report all forms of student financial assistance as a "source of income"; that amount is subtracted in total or in prorated amounts from total allowable benefits. Further, applications for public assistance programs tend to lump all forms of student aid in one category, including student loans that eventually must be paid back. A typical question for applicants on state public assistance forms asks, "Is anyone getting a scholarship, fellowship, or student loans or grants?" (Michigan Department of Social Services 1985). And applicants have no option to differentiate between need-based and non-need-based student aid. Questions regarding student aid tend to be the same for monthly reporting requirements, particularly for food stamps, Aid to Families with Dependent Children (AFDC), Supplemental Social Security Income, and Public Housing Assistance. Recipients of food stamps are required to differentiate "total amount of grants, scholarships, or loans" and "tuition and mandatory fees,"* which

*U.S. Department of Agriculture 1983. Application for Food Stamps, form FNS-385 (7-83).

results in student aid money not going toward tuition and mandatory fees being counted against food stamp benefits.

College students receiving benefits from unemployment insurance, the Job Training Partnership Act, and public housing programs confront additional financial hardships. The Work Incentive (WIN) programs required for unemployment insurance, for example, generally do not consider the number of hours worked in the College Work Study program as meeting the 20-hour-per-week requirement for receiving unemployment benefits. Students attending school have been denied or cut off from unemployment benefits because they are perceived as "not available for work." Recipients in public housing assistance programs generally pay higher rents when student aid benefits are calculated as a "source of income."

In most public welfare programs, particularly AFDC, states are given considerable discretion in setting rules for recipients because most states provide joint funding. Thus, states tend to differ in how they establish eligibility to receive student aid. At times, the standard-of-living allowances in student aid programs are higher than the poverty-level standard used in public assistance programs. Furthermore, the College Board concludes, "the complex, often changing, and frequently confusing regulations governing AFDC may be interpreted differently from county to county and sometimes even from caseworker to caseworker" (Hansen and Franklin 1984, p. 2).

In a related concern, an overlooked consequence of the sweeping congressional changes in the 1981 social security laws, which included eliminating student aid for survivors, is the adverse impact on women (Webster and Perry 1983). Full-time students who were children of workers entitled to full benefits and were between the ages of 18 and 21 were eligible for student aid, generally averaging $300 per month. The primary argument advanced to justify elimination of this benefit was that $50 million would be added to the appropriation for Pell Grants to compensate for the loss. Now, more than five years later, nothing has yet been added to Pell Grants. Women, who are more likely to outlive their husbands, thus face the virtual inability to send children to school when a husband's income stops at death.

*[This] results in student aid money not going toward tuition and mandatory fees being counted against food stamp benefits.*

**Graduate Education**

Continued obstacles prevent the progress of women in research. In fact, the depressed state of the academic job market, combined with demographic changes, rapidly escalating costs, and reduced financial aid, discourages outstanding students from continuing their studies. The grim situation of low participation and lack of economic support appears to be the rule of thumb for women (National Commission on Student Financial Assistance 1983b). Available data on major student aid programs generally do not distinguish between undergraduate and graduate assistance; thus, it becomes difficult to assess the distribution of federal, state, and institutional dollars. Moreover, major national research projects designed to assess needs and student aid for graduate students have failed to take gender into account (Butler-Nalin, Sanderson, and Redman 1983; Flamer, Horch, and Davis 1982).

The distribution of graduate assistantships, fellowships, and other awards is characterized by great decentralization, and individual departments have great autonomy. Most of these awards are neither available through nor monitored by an institution's student financial aid office but are generally dispersed by department chairs (often chair*men*), and substantial differences exist among schools within a single university. According to the National Women's Law Center, "If a department is controlled by faculty who believe women have no place in the discipline or profession, distribution of graduate financial aid may well reflect that bias. Expectations that women will leave the workforce for periods of childbearing or childrearing may also influence the distribution of graduate fellowships or other aid" (Campbell et al. 1983, pp. 4-4–4-7).

Thus, one major factor contributing to attrition and to low rates of retention and completion stems from the attitudes of faculty toward granting financial aid, which are closely related to women's ability to study full time. Further, women tend to take longer to get their degrees and drop out at a higher rate (Rees 1976).

*For women, graduate study poses problems that are different from those encountered at the undergraduate level and that sharpen the conflicts between traditional roles and alternative roles. The typical age for women in*

*graduate school is also the age when society makes its
greatest demands for traditional role behavior. Women
between twenty-two and thirty both expect and are
expected to be wives whose husbands are establishing
their own careers and also to be mothers of preschool
children. This traditional role frequently conflicts with
the student and scholar role. . . . Few would maintain
that a master's degree in any field is necessary or even
desirable for women who expect to live out their lives as
wives and mothers, and many people would argue that a
Ph.D. is a downright disadvantage. Thus graduate education for women is more controversial than college education. It is also much more difficult because the women
who embark on this path run into the barriers erected by
the broader society as well as those erected by graduate
and professional schools* (Cross 1976, pp. 37–38).

Another critical issue regarding graduate education is the
disproportionate balance of men holding significantly more
research assistantships—as opposed to teaching assistantships—especially in the rapidly growing fields of math, science, and computer technology. Research assistantships,
primarily federally funded, are generally awarded by a
department chair or the research director of a federal project rather than by a student aid administrator. Testimony
before the National Commission on Student Financial
Assistance noted:

*A research assistantship contributes to the quality of
graduate education. It serves to integrate the student
into the profession. It serves to teach him or her the sort
of nontechnical elements of the profession. You learn
how the grant mechanisms work. You become in the sciences, in a very important way, integrated into the
research group, which no other form of support provides. So we see rather gradually, insidiously, differen-
tiation taking place where women are expected to do a
disproportionately higher share of undergraduate teaching, which takes them away from the company of their
colleagues and faculty and puts them into a different
environment with young students, while male students
are working with faculty and regarded as colleagues.
. . . They are likely to have more opportunities to publish*

*before they actually finish their Ph.D.s. They are likely*
*to have subsidized travel, attend meetings, have oppor-*
*tunities to be introduced to people in other institutions*
(Hornig 1983, pp. 243–44).

Moreover, while graduate students with teaching assistantships are often classified as college faculty, the positions
are seldom if ever tenure-track positions.

The field of education itself merits a close examination of
differences in graduate support between sexes in view of
the fact that high-paying jobs in postsecondary as well as
elementary and secondary education are virtually limited
to males. Currently, only 8 percent of college presidents
and 2 percent of school district superintendents are women
(Jones and Montenago 1982; Shavlik 1984). Furthermore,
over 50 percent of male school district superintendents and
fewer than 2 percent of female superintendents have doctoral degrees. Lack of financial resources for advanced
training (internships, assistantships, fully paid leaves of
absence, reimbursement of travel and expenses, for example) and lack of opportunities for professional development
are primary barriers in obtaining the skills, credentials, and
degrees required for higher-paying jobs in education (Shakeshaft 1985).[1]

The real financial problems, however, are not seen in the
data collected from graduate students, because minority
women and independent women with children in particular
with their limited resources do not even think of applying
to graduate school. Particular attention needs to address:
(1) the possibility that loan burdens for women may be proportionately greater because their anticipated lifetime earnings are smaller; (2) cultural factors that discourage many
women from considering careers in science and engineering; and (3) biases in favor of men in awarding fellowships
and research assistantships (National Commission on Student Financial Assistance 1983b).

1. Yet management internships have high price tags. The University of
California estimates the average cost of a six-month staff internship is
$16,200, while the average cost for a management internship is $24,442
(University of California 1985).

## Corporate Benefits That Pay Tuition

Increasingly, courses for men enrolled in graduate programs are partially or totally paid for by their employers. Characteristically, it is not happening for women. Many types of tuition aid plans have become fringe benefits of one's job, primarily as a way to upgrade and improve job skills and as a step toward promotion, yet women use such benefits much less frequently than men (Abramovitz 1977).

While men and women share many barriers to using tuition aid (low job status, limited job opportunities, cost, lack of time, program regulations, and attitudes about the benefits of additional education), other obstacles limit women in particular. The position of women at the bottom of the job and income ladders, the effect of sex-role stereotyping on occupational expectations, and the effect of responsibilities at home on their free time contribute to even lower use of tuition aid by women and justify particular emphasis on improving their participation (Abramovitz 1977).

A recent study by the U.S. Department of Education suggests that working women confront many barriers in tuition benefit programs in the Fortune 1000 corporations (O'Neill 1984). First, as employees move into top management positions, their job descriptions become more generalized, thereby having access to a wider range of "job-related" training options. As more women tend to work in nonmanagerial positions with more restricted job descriptions, they thus have fewer job-related training options. Second, few if any corporate tuition programs allow expenses for child care.

Furthermore, corporations not having tuition reimbursement plans tend to be concentrated in the two industries—airlines and retail sales—that hire mostly women in low-level positions. Many companies do not extend eligibility to hourly workers. Although some hourly workers are covered by separate union contracts, most hourly workers, who are predominantly women, have no access to tuition benefits (U.S. Department of Labor 1984). And 86 percent of the corporations surveyed reimburse their employees for courses taken only after they achieve a satisfactory grade. Because more women fall into the lower income categories, the inability to provide tuition and registration fees upfront has a significant adverse effect. Lower-income employees are doubly disadvantaged when they can afford neither the initial payment of tuition nor the risk of failure (O'Neill 1984).

### Child Care

A significant cost of attending college for many women is that of child care, yet student aid policies are inconsistent and unclear—in fact, generally nonexistent—as to what allowances may be claimed. Federal regulations for the largest aid programs, Pell Grants and GSLs, for example, do not allow the cost of child care, while regulations for campus-based programs provide for "reasonably incurred" expenses. Furthermore, the College Work Study program makes no allowances for payment of child care while a student is working (usually 20 hours a week) in addition to costs for child care incurred during the time spent in a classroom. Allocations for administering campus-based programs do not allow for subsidizing campus child care services for students, nor do fiscal operations reports provide information on university subsidies for child care.

The largest sources of federal funding for day care are indirect—the tax credit allowed for child care on individual returns and tax deductions taken by employers who provide some form of day care assistance to employees (U.S. Congress 1984a). Yet only "work-related expenses" qualify for the credit, and the credit may be taken only by a married couple with a full-time "student-spouse." Moreover, the IRS's definition of full-time student states that "a student who attends school only at night is not a full-time student."* And costs for child care may be deducted only when an individual is working, not when he or she is going to school. Consequently, these requirements prevent many women from taking advantage of the credit for child care.

Corporate tax writeoffs for child care tend to cover only work-related expenses, not education or staff development. Further, costs of child care are generally not allowable in corporate benefit programs that pay tuition. Although many corporations are beginning to recognize the need for child care among increasing numbers of working parents, much effort is still needed to include child care in corporate programs covering tuition and in private partner-

*IRS publication 503, *Child and Disabled Dependent Care*, 1984, p. 1.

ships with local universities. Doing so would pay off for employers: Those with some form of child care program receive a return on their investment in the form of increased productivity and loyalty, enhanced public image, improved recruitment, and reduced turnover, absenteeism, and tardiness (The White House 1984).

For recipients of AFDC, the payments toward child care allow only for time spent in the classroom and do not include hours spent traveling to and from child care centers or to and from school, in the library, or in field work. Recipients of AFDC must also deduct money not covering tuition and fees from the monthly food stamp budget. Such trends place great pressure on women to enroll part time rather than full time and result in higher dropout rates for female students with children.

**Minority Women**
Reports and research on minority participation in higher education and in student aid programs have failed to address the critical educational needs of minority women. Women from racial or religious minorities and handicapped women continually confront multiple barriers—race, religion, handicapping condition, sex—to equal education opportunity, yet at the same time, each minority group must be viewed in light of its particular cultural, economic, political, and educational characteristics. For example, while Native American females graduate from high school at the lowest rate (8 percent), Japanese-American women finish high school at a rate of 99 percent. Nearly all minority women are disproportionately disadvantaged, however. These multiple barriers are most salient in work earnings, where no group of minority women's earnings are equal to their male counterparts (Bailey 1983; Lewis et al. 1985).

The problem of meeting educational costs for minority teenage mothers is acute. As more than half of the 12 million children who live in families headed by women are living in poverty, increasing proportions of minority children in families headed by minority women are growing up in poverty. Addressing the financial needs of these women is imperative, particularly including sufficient child care and transportation costs as allowable costs in student aid formulas. Teenage parents are only half as likely as those who bear children after age 20 to enroll in college, and those who become pregnant after 20 are four to five times more likely to have completed college than teen parents. Families headed by teen parents are seven times as likely to live in poverty as all households in the country. In fact, the age at which a young mother first gives birth is one of the strongest, if not the strongest, influence on the level of education she will attain (Guttmacher Institute 1985).

Black Americans, the largest minority group, continue to face significant problems in achieving access to higher education in the United States (National Advisory Committee 1980). In 1970, about 30 percent of black families were headed by women; by 1980, 42 percent were headed by women. More than half lacked high school diplomas, three-fifths lacked jobs, and almost two-fifths of female-headed families received welfare. The current poverty rate for households headed by black females is 45 percent (National Urban League 1984).

The problem of illiteracy hurts minority and migrant women disproportionately more than any other group (Kozol 1985; Spero 1985). Such women are held back farther as a consequence of high rates of teenage pregnancy, unemployment, and unequal job earnings. Clearly the problems of minority women have significant implications for college recruiting, disseminating information about financial aid, and partnerships between high schools and colleges.

One program particularly helpful to minority women is the Special Services Grants for Disadvantaged Students program under Title III of the Higher Education Act. Every institution receiving a Special Services Grant must assure that each participant enrolled in the project will receive "sufficient financial assistance to meet that participant's full financial need. It is incumbent upon the project to work with the participants *and* the institution to see that this assurance is met" (34 CFR 646). This federal program is particularly important to women: It served 104,696 women (compared to 76,672 men) throughout fiscal year 1981–82. Despite these impressive numbers, however, the national average amount received was only $352. It is not known whether men or women receive higher average awards, because that information is not collected, but a recent study concludes that "the absence of adequate research data on minority women is a measure of the absence of educational equity'' (Lewis et al. 1985, p. 380).

One exemplary practice at the graduate level for promoting minority women is that of the National Consortium for Graduate Degrees for Minorities in Engineering, a joint effort by universities and private industry to increase the numbers of blacks, Mexican-Americans, Puerto Ricans, and American Indians earning graduate degrees in engineering. This organization comprises 42 leading high-technology companies and research laboratories and 40 top-rated engineering schools (Friedland 1983).

*The current poverty rate for households headed by black females is 45 percent.*

### Assessment of Financial Need

Studies of education costs and resources for full-time undergraduates in three states found many differences between men and women in the patterns of financial resources available to pay for college costs. Based on a sample of almost 29,000 undergraduates in 241 colleges and universities, differences between men and women appear in total resources available to pay for college, in the amounts and percentages derived from different sources, and in the way financial aid is distributed among students (Davis 1977).

Since student aid programs began, the question of how to justly and equitably distribute available resources to worthy students has been a source of much debate, controversy, and lobbying. Issues surrounding such factors as ability to pay, vertical and horizontal equity, expected contributions from the family and the student, standard maintenance allowances, and students' expense budgets have perplexed student aid officials (Berkshire 1985; Binder 1983; Case 1983). And the financial needs of women as nontraditional students are not given adequate attention.

Basic assumptions and practices used to calculate ''financial need'' tend not to consider issues of gender related to ''total family contribution'' (or ''expected family contribution''), the foundation upon which most federal and nonfederal student aid is awarded. The amount, determined by formula, is the sum a student and his or her family can contribute toward college costs. The figure is important because it is subtracted from the ''cost of education'' in determining financial need; however, unusual expenses, such as child care, many times are not considered. Consequently, parents' and spouses' support for education is noticeably different for men and women. Parents of women contribute more than expected in relation to amounts contributed by parents of men (Bob 1977; Davis 1977; Leslie 1977). And they contribute more because they have to; it does not appear that parents of women contribute more because of a greater ability to contribute.

For nearly 65 percent of women—versus 47 percent for men—parental aid is a major source of support. And financial support from spouses is especially important for married women, not only in terms of actual dollars provided but also because major support from a spouse can determine whether a woman will persist and complete college.

*On a more subtle level, spouses who are ambivalent or resentful about their partner's attending college may provide only sporadic or little support. Whatever the explanation, providing only minor support may create uncertainties or conflicts that militate against completing college. If nothing else, married students might be well advised to reach a clear understanding about financial support from their spouses before they finalize plans to enroll in college* (Astin 1975, p. 9).

Several systems have emerged to assess income and financial resources, analyze needs, and identify potential sources of financial aid. Since 1975, the "uniform methodology" has become a nationally accepted standard for determining a student's need and eligibility for most federal (except Pell Grants and GSLs), state, and institutional financial aid (Berkshire 1985). What appears to be a very straightforward determination of financial need (total family contribution subtracted from the student's cost of attendance at a given institution) is not so straightforward, however. Inherent in the uniform methodology are assumptions about students' financial resources that create a disproportionate effect on women. The calculation of "expected earnings," for example, is the same for both males and females, even though national statistics clearly show that women earn less than men per hour and research shows that women are not as able as men to rely on savings to cover college costs (Leslie 1982; U.S. Department of Labor 1984). Expected earnings are inappropriately based on summer earnings, even though men and women earn significantly different amounts, rather than on earnings acquired during the school year (Maxwell 1984). Further, the uniform methodology tends to be uniform in name only, as many aid officers use much discretion in the distribution of financial aid.

**Effect of Student Aid on Choice of Career**
Current student aid policies operate in a vacuum, providing no incentives for universities to promote degree programs in which graduates (especially women and minorities) acquire a higher probability of landing adequately paid and personally satisfying jobs. Neither are federal incentives provided to develop corporate and business partnerships with federal student aid programs so as to ensure a more appropriate match between postsecondary education programs and the labor market (Moran 1983). Furthermore, student aid policies have not been sufficiently adapted to the fact that many women are now part-time or independent students and that the number is growing rapidly. Considerable attention has focused recently on high unemployment and underemployment among college graduates, yet postsecondary institutions and student aid policies simply have not met the demands of the constantly changing labor market.

Student aid policy could be a very useful mechanism for providing incentives to schools and corporations to change the occupational distribution of women. Although women make up 43.3 percent of the work force, they are still clustered in the lowest-paying jobs. Some 34 percent are in clerical jobs, 27 percent in service occupations—waitresses, retail sales personnel, and medical aides. Even the 18 percent listed as professionals are believed to be mostly teachers and nurses earning relatively low pay (Brooks 1983). Further, the current deindustrialization of our country necessitates not only a redistribution of women into other career areas but also a stronger emphasis on retraining and lifelong learning (Bluestone and Harrison 1982). Student aid policy can encourage women to develop marketable skills needed in the labor force. Current advertisements call for people to become field service engineers, satellite communication specialists, financial program control analysts, telemarketing representatives, systems application programmers, computer data base designers, artificial intelligence specialists, systems engineers, and tele-communication network scientists.* It is well known that women do not receive bachelor's degrees in these areas, let alone master's or doctoral degrees.

In fact, the College Work Study (CWS) program and the State Student Incentive Grant (SSIG) program, perhaps two of the most favorable aid programs for improving career choices and work experience for women, actually include regulatory barriers to facilitating career development. Regulations for CWS, for example, specify that students in the program can use the services of a job location and development project only when in school, not after they graduate. Further, eligibility for CWS is restricted to full-time students (34 CFR 675). The SSIG program has a cap on matching contributions from the states.

### Disseminating Information and Targeting Recipients
Obtaining the right kind of financial information at the right time is the critical dimension that determines, for many students, whether or not they will attend college; in fact, low-income students usually apply for college as a consequence of having been provided adequate information about student aid (Carroll 1983; Gruss and Hauptman 1985; Stelk 1983). Greater effort is therefore needed in targeting information about student aid to high school students. The National Commission on Student Financial Assistance, the National Association of College Admissions Counselors, and the National Student Aid Coalition, in particular, have channeled much of their resources toward research and the development of improved strategies for disseminating information.

Targeting student aid information toward women is a recognized need: Sex-role stereotypes and traditional attitudes block women from progressing toward degrees in higher education. In fact, a lack of targeted information on financial assistance "[acts] as a deterrent for many potential students, [has] a negative impact upon access and retention of low-income and minority students, and [limits] . . . [choices] among institutions" (Stelk 1983, p. 3).

Many women do not pursue postsecondary education simply because they believe they cannot afford it; thus,

*The Washington Post 20 October 1983.*

they do not exert any effort to learn about institutions and careers. Information generally reaches higher-income students and males rather than lower-income students and females. Thus, "those with the greatest financial need remain uninformed about aid programs, [which] may contribute to a decline in enrollments" (Stelk 1983, p. 9). A recognized need exists for high school guidance counselors and college recruiters to watch closely for high achievers who for whatever reason do not apply to college or talk about college plans. Such students tend to be from low-income groups and do not have the self-confidence that they will be accepted into college. Knowledge of available student aid can be a determining factor in a student's realizing his or her academic potential. More high schools need to be equipped with expanded information resources, including computer-assisted scholarship searches free of charge to students.

**Progress of Title IX**
An overlooked issue in the debate about Title IX and the interpretation of the Supreme Court's ruling in *Grove City College* v. *Bell* [687 F.2d 684 (3d Cir. 1982), *aff'd*, 104 S.Ct. 1211 (1984)] is that of financial assistance for students. Title IX of the Education Amendments of 1972 was intended to eliminate discrimination on the basis of gender in most education programs and activities receiving federal financial assistance, and financial aid is recognized as one area that is particularly vulnerable to differential treatment on the basis of gender. Regulations require that postsecondary institutions providing financial assistance to any of their students may not provide different amounts or types of assistance, limit eligibility for assistance, apply different criteria, or otherwise discriminate on the basis of sex. Further, an institution's application for federal funds must be accompanied by an assurance that financial aid will be administered in compliance with regulations for Title IX. The U.S. Office for Civil Rights's enforcement practices, however, do not include student financial assistance as a category for compliance reviews, and no decisions on financial aid from the perspective of equitable distribution of dollars have been handed down by the courts. Ironically, federal judges have heard substantial legal debate about whether or not Pell Grants in particular are to be

considered as federal assistance to an institution, thus requiring compliance with Title IX.

Guidelines in table 9 established by the U.S. Office for Civil Rights for analysis of student financial assistance in determining compliance with Title VI of the Civil Rights Act of 1964 and Title IX "assume" that institutions maintain data regarding the provision of financial assistance to students by race, national origin, and gender. These guidelines state, however, that "if an institution does not maintain such data, the failure to do so is not a violation of Title VI or Title IX" (U.S. Department of Education 1981, p. 2). Thus, institutions generally do not maintain data about gender for federal funding, because they are not required to do so.

In the historic *Grove City* v. *Bell,* the U.S. Supreme Court ruled that the receipt of Pell Grants (BEOGs), a federal grant program designed to address a national need and

## TABLE 9

### DATA REQUIRED FOR ANALYSIS OF FINANCIAL ASSISTANCE

**I. Merit-Based Financial Assistance**
- *A. Comparison of Students Receiving Financial Assistance*
  - Summary data of total enrollment by race, sex, and national origin, broken down by students receiving and not receiving financial assistance by race, sex, and national origin
- *B. Comparison of Average Size and Type of Financial Assistance*
  - Individual records or a list of all awards
  - Race, sex, and/or national origin of each student receiving financial assistance
  - Source of each award
  - Type of assistantship or employment performed
- *C. Analysis of Criteria to Determine Which Students Receive Merit-Based Financial Assistance*
  - Criteria, guidelines, or standards used to determine which students receive financial assistance
  - Application of each student who applied or was considered for financial assistance (test scores, grades, recommendations)
  - Any evaluation or rating used by the school, department, or program for determining which students receive financial assistance

Table 9 (continued)

**II. Need-Based Financial Assistance**

    *A. Comparison of Students Receiving Financial Assistance*
- See "A" above.

    *B. Comparison of Average Size and Type of Financial Assistance*
- See "B" above.

    *C. Replication of the Process by Which Need Is Determined*
- Guidelines or standards used by the school for determining a student's need
- For each student in the sample, the completed Graduate and Professional School Financial Aid Service form (or form provided by other services)
- For each student in the sample, the actual award made by the school, including the components (for example, scholarships, grants, loans) of each award and the source of each component

    *D. Comparison of the Elements by Which Need Is Determined and Met*
- For each student in the sample, the parents' contribution, the student's contribution, need, award, and extent of the student's "self-help" contribution

An institution's not maintaining data on students receiving financial assistance by race, national origin, or sex is not a violation of Title VI or Title IX. Institutions may be requested to maintain such data, in accord with departmental requirements, under 34 CFR 100.(6) and 34 CFR 106.71. It is not necessary to personally identify any student.

*Source:* U.S. Department of Education 1981, p 12.

enable financially disadvantaged students to attend postsecondary institutions, "does not trigger institution-wide coverage under Title IX. In purpose and effect, BEOGs represent federal financial assistance to the College's own financial aid program, and it is that program that may properly be regulated under Title IX" (p. 1211). This decision has inadvertently required federal and university officials to examine standards and expectations in helping women finance postsecondary education, an issue about equitable policy that has virtually been ignored. Congressional hearings and heated debates intended to overturn this ruling have not addressed the Supreme Court's directive to review student aid. Further, initial interpretations have emphasized only the "student aid office," not the "student aid program" mandated by the Supreme Court. This distinction is essential because many awards of student aid—for example, athletic scholarships, graduate internships, endowments, scholarships from the private sector—neither filter through nor are reported by an institution's student aid office.

To date, institutions have not been held accountable for equitable distribution of scholarships, graduate fellowships, state grants, or other forms of student assistance. Much of the problem lies not only in lack of enforcing Title IX but also in practices of distributing student aid—the decentralization of distribution, the lack of available reports detailing the distribution of student aid by gender, and promises to maintain "confidentiality" in an effort to acquire family financial information. Many students view the matter of financial aid as a personal issue and are reluctant to discuss the nature of their aid with others. As a result, few students, administrators, or state and national policy makers are aware of the way other students in similar financial circumstances are treated or the way male and female students fare as distinct groups (Campbell et al. 1983). Federal judges are known to perceive Title IX cases as frivolous and, looking for ways to clear their overloaded dockets, refuse to hear Title IX cases (Gladen 1983).

For issues of equity in education other than student financial assistance—admissions, intercollegiate athletics, dress and appearance codes, sexual harassment, student activities—Title IX has actually marked tremendous progress in achieving initial steps toward educational opportunity. Title IX also reflects the social revolution taking place throughout the country and substantial changes in attitudes among both men and women about the provision of equity. This federal legislation has been quite successful in launching the first major initiative in prohibiting discrimination based on sex, thus enabling women to make substantial strides in pursuing higher degrees, particularly in nontraditional programs like science, engineering, law, and medicine. It is no longer news that women are being admitted to prestigious law schools, playing in college sports, and enrolling in nontraditional career programs; the question now is whether women will be able to pay for higher education, increasing their chances of earning salaries of comparable worth.

## The Participation of Women in Developing Policy

Improving women's receipt of student aid tends to be contingent on women's active involvement in and recognition during policy deliberations. The very existence of Title IX, for example, is attributed to the commitment, power, and leadership of Edith Greene, who chaired the House Subcommittee on Postsecondary Education during the passage of the Education Amendments of 1972 (Gladieux and Wolanin 1976). Influential commissions and blue ribbon task forces on higher education are more likely to recognize the needs of women when women are involved. The first and second Newman Task Forces are good examples. The first Newman Task Force, established in the early 1970s by HEW Secretary Elliot Richardson, was comprised of one female and eight males; its final report devoted a whole chapter to barriers to equity for women in postsecondary education, concluding:

> *The unique role of higher education gives it extraordinary leverage to either help or hurt women's chances for equality of opportunity. When colleges and universities deny women the chance to gain skills and credentials, they increase the likelihood that women will not receive equal opportunities in all other social institutions for the rest of their lives* (Newman 1971, p. 51).

The second Newman Task Force, created to recommend specific strategies for addressing the problems the first task force had identified, included no females. And the final report makes no mention of equity for women (Newman 1973).

# HOW ARE WOMEN PAYING FOR COLLEGE?

Nearly all of the debate, research, and lobbying on the distribution of student aid have concentrated on percentages and amounts of funds received by type of institution—four-year public, two-year public, independent, and proprietary (Andersen 1986; Breneman and Nelson 1981; Congressional Research Service 1985; El-Khawas 1983; Hyde 1979; National Institute of Independent Colleges and Universities 1983; Stampen 1985; Wilms 1983). And some of the more difficult questions have been overlooked: What is the distribution of student aid among women? What is the nature of their aid packages? How do women fare in student employment programs? Do women receive equal shares of institutionally funded and corporate-funded student aid? What is the nature of their cumulative debt? With over $21 billion invested each year in all forms of student aid, these questions need to be addressed. Other financial resources—for example, the student's and the family's contributions from savings and summer earnings—also need examination.

The definition of financial need in federal programs is "the difference between a student's cost of attendance and his or her expected family contributions," yet what appears to be a simple and straightforward way to assess needs actually has created subtle barriers for women. Women have a greater need for student aid, because they are more likely to enroll as independent, unclassified, or part-time students and because they are more likely to hold primary responsibilities for child care. They are apt to incur additional costs for enrolling in remedial math and science courses as a result of societal biases frequently encountered in elementary and secondary schools expecting women not to excel in those subjects. Women constitute a disproportionate number of transfer students, especially from community colleges to four-year institutions but also as a consequence of moving with husbands whose jobs are relocated. Postsecondary institutions frequently do not accept all coursework completed at a previous school and require additional courses for meeting departmental requirements for graduation.

Despite evidence of greater need, women receive less financial aid than comparable males, and their student aid packages present greater financial burdens. Of immediate concern are low-income women. Given that many aid pro-

*Women have a greater need for student aid, because they are more likely to enroll as independent, unclassified, or part-time students and because [of] child care.*

grams are based on formulas, a necessary unit of analysis then becomes the formula itself. While significant effort has gone into developing federal statutes and regulations intended to be fair and equitable, the ultimate factor guaranteeing women's access to financial support is clearly the commitment, leadership, and knowledge of officials at postsecondary institutions. Actual practices many times are not the same as written policies at all levels of government, and subtle differences in women's receipt of student aid are not so subtle after taking a closer look at differences by income levels, investigating restrictive regulatory policies and practices of lenders, and discovering how institutions sometimes use discretionary authority inappropriately in the distribution of financial aid. (Table 10, pp. 46–8, points out a few trends in the distribution of financial aid by gender.)

Another troublesome point deserving consideration is the fact that current data bases tend to be very limited and simply do not provide answers to difficult problems. While much progress has recently been made to assess the impact of policy through research, much work is still needed. Few data bases funded by private and federal sources have emerged, yet the few that exist are frequently used for congressional lobbying, thus many times emphasizing special interests. The most significant question has been how student aid is distributed among private, public, and proprietary institutions.

Major databases receiving federal funds include *The High School and Beyond Survey* and *The Cooperative Institutional Research Program.* Private foundations and higher education associations have additionally invested significant funds in the *Public School Recipient Files* and the *Private School Recipient Files,* and the U.S. Department of Education has funded a wide variety of studies using several databases. Inconsistent and noncomparable data, however, are "damaging to the accuracy and timeliness of institutional and state-level planning and monitoring efforts, and to the appropriateness of public policies promulgated on the basis of misleading, incomplete, or contradictory data" (U.S. Department of Education 1984h, p. 20). More recently, the U.S. Department of Education launched a multimillion dollar national survey of student aid that will build on what was learned from previous studies and will be available during the next few years.

Meanwhile, the particular financial concerns confronting women are nowhere addressed in the popular research on student aid. This chapter describes issues of gender by type of program and reports research findings where they do exist. Programs of particular interest to women include the Guaranteed Student Loan program, College Work Study, National Direct Student Loans, Pell Grants, Supplemental Educational Opportunity Grants, state scholarships and grants, and athletic and military scholarships. Job training assistance programs are increasingly important; they include cooperative education, the Job Training Partnership Act, and—most rapidly growing—corporate benefits that pay tuition.

## Guaranteed Student Loans

The Guaranteed Student Loan program assists students in securing federally subsidized loans to help them finance their postsecondary education. It is the largest ($3.7 billion in FY 1985), most complex, fastest growing, and most controversial of all federal student aid programs (Clohan 1985; National Council of Higher Education Loan Programs 1984). The federal government does not actually make loans; instead it pays insurance premiums and special allowances to lenders—credit unions, multistate banks, local savings and loan institutions, and community banks— to encourage their participation and pays interest subsidies on behalf of students until they begin repayment.

The GSL program is frequently portrayed as a financial time bomb: Bankruptcy claims for recipients of GSLs were estimated to have increased nearly $3 million from 1983 to 1984, from $21 million to $24 million. Further, the costs of underwriting the bankruptcies continue to rise. In 1982, the U.S. Department of Education paid out $14 million for bankruptcy subsidies, compared to $9 million in 1978 (U.S. Department of Education 1984i). Costs for defaults for FY 1984 were $793.9 million, an increase of about $308 million over the previous year (Clohan 1985). And GSLs show the highest rates of fraud and abuse (U.S. Department of Education 1984i).

### Analysis of participation rates and average awards
Women's participation in the GSL program does not reflect their rates of enrollment and is disproportionately low, par-

# TABLE 10
## DISTRIBUTION OF STUDENT AID BY GENDER[a]

| | Public School Recipient File Male | Public School Recipient File Female | Private School Recipient File Male | Private School Recipient File Female | Top Twenty Academic Rank Male | Top Twenty Academic Rank Female | Leslie Male | Leslie Female | Freshman Norms Fall 1985 Male | Freshman Norms Fall 1985 Female |
|---|---|---|---|---|---|---|---|---|---|---|
| **Own Savings/Earnings** | | | | | | | | | | |
| Aid per recipient | $390 | $345 | $665 | $386 | | | $1,055 | $680 | | |
| Percent participating | | | – | – | | | | | 15.4 | 9.7 |
| Percent of total expenses | | | 9.3 | 6.0 | | | | | 6.4 | 5.5 |
| **Support of Family/Friends** | | | | | | | | | | |
| Aid per recipient | | | $217 | $102 | | | $126 | $214 | | |
| Percent participating | | | – | – | | | | | 33.8 | 50.6 |
| Percent of total expenses | | | 3.0 | 1.6 | | | | | | |
| **Scholarships/Grants** | | | | | | | | | | |
| Aid per recipient | $1,373 | $1,236 | $2,637 | $2,821 | | | $98 | $32 | | |
| Percent participating | | | – | – | | | | | | |
| Percent of total expenses | | | 36.8 | 43.8 | | | | | | |
| **Total Loans** | | | | | | | | | | |
| Aid per recipient | $961 | $712 | $1,195 | $927 | | | $47 | $15 | | |
| Percent participating | | | – | – | | | | | | |
| Percent of total expenses | | | 16.7 | 14.4 | | | | | | |

| | | | | |
|---|---|---|---|---|
| **Pell Grant** | | | | |
| Aid per recipient | $761 | $711 | | |
| Percent participating | 23.8 | 25.1 | 8.9 | 10.2 |
| Percent of cost covered | 14.28 | 13.65 | | |
| **Guaranteed Student Loan** | | | | |
| Aid per recipient | $1,878 | $1,842 | | |
| Percent participating | 27.5 | 28.8 | 19.2 | 19.6 |
| Percent of cost covered | 35.25 | 35.36 | | |
| **College Work Study** | | | | |
| Aid per recipient | $825 | $763 | | |
| Percent participating | 16.2 | 19.7 | 2.7 | 3.2 |
| Percent of cost covered | 15.50 | 14.64 | | |
| **SEOG** | | | | |
| Aid per recipient | $750 | $676 | | |
| Percent participating | 7.3 | 7.1 | 1.6 | 1.6 |
| Percent of cost covered | 14.08 | 12.97 | | |
| **NDSL** | | | | |
| Aid per recipient | $1,098 | $1,124 | | |
| Percent participating | 10.3 | 10.6 | 3.1 | 3.4 |
| Percent of cost covered | 20.61 | 21.58 | | |
| **State Scholarships/Grants** | | | | |
| Aid per recipient | $715 | $699 | | |
| Percent participating | 23.4 | 25.9 | 4.6 | 4.7 |
| Percent of cost covered | 13.43 | 13.41 | | |

**TABLE 10 CONTINUED**

| | Public School Recipient File | | Private School Recipient File | | Top Twenty Academic Rank | | Leslie | | Freshman Norms Fall 1985 | |
|---|---|---|---|---|---|---|---|---|---|---|
| | *Male* | *Female* | *Male* | *Female* | *Male* | *Female* | *Male* | *Female* | *Male* | *Female* |
| **Other** | | | | | | | | | | |
| Aid per recipient | $258 | $228 | | | | | $69.38 | $33.58 | | |
| Percent participating | | | | | | | 2.3 | 1.1 | 1.6 | 0.7 |
| | | | | | | | | | | |
| **Total Resources** | | | | | | | | | | |
| Aid per recipient | $2,982 | $2,521 | $6,723 | $5,648 | | | $1,326 | $942 | | |
| Percent participating | | | – | – | | | | | | |
| Percent of total expenses | | | 93.8 | 87.64 | | | | | | |
| | | | | | | | | | | |
| **Unmet Need** | | | | | | | | | | |
| Balance | | | ($446) | ($799) | | | | | | |
| Percent of total expenses | | | – 6.2 | – 12.4 | | | | | | |

[a]Selected data from major studies:
Public School Recipient File (1982): independent students attending four-year and two-year public institutions. Survey of actual student aid records.
Private School Recipient File (1982): dependent, undergraduate students attending private institutions (income level under $6,000). Survey of actual student aid records.
Cooperative Institutional Research Program (1982): full-time freshmen only. Based on income levels of $20,000 to $30,000.
Leslie 1982: NIE Higher Education Indicators project; part-time students (NLS data for 1975–76).
Freshman Norms (1985): full-time freshmen only, entering 365 institutions (all types).

ticularly for low-income women (see table 11). Low-income women tend to receive GSLs at nearly *half* the rate of comparable males (9 percent versus 15.6 percent), while high-income females have a higher participation rate than comparable males (18 percent versus 16.9 percent) (U.S. Department of Education 1983).

Throughout the history of the GSL program, charges have been levied that certain students tend to be denied loans—out-of-state students, students enrolling in less-than-two-year programs, those with no previous relationship with the lender, and students enrolling in proprietary schools (National Commission on Student Financial Assistance 1984).

High tuitions and the necessity of relying on one's own resources mean that the need for loans at many schools is large and growing. Women tend to rely more on loans because they have to. In the absence of sufficient grants and work study programs, women increasingly must incur large college debts if they want to complete school. Moreover, more women are deciding to attend graduate school, further increasing individual debt, and they may be borrowing smaller amounts than needed from more costly sources (credit cards, for example). Women may be unwilling to commit themselves to student loans because they anticipate low future income (Johnson 1983). This "hidden demand" for student loans from those entering underpaid professions raises important policy questions, and it may partially explain the differences between low-income and high-income women's participation.

*Policy issues*
Much attention has been focused on rising defaults and student borrowers' willingness to repay loans, but little attention has been given to *ability* to repay, a function of both the size of the debt and the requirements for repayment in relation to a borrower's income over the term of the loan. The average annual salary of women with GSLs to repay is $17,040, while that for males is $23,093 (Boyd and Martin 1986, p. 22). Although women have lower participation rates than males while in school, the participation rate of women who are repaying loans is higher (57.6 percent), suggesting that males are able to repay loans sooner after graduation. Women who are repaying loans say they wish

## TABLE 11
## PERCENTAGE OF PARTICIPATION IN GSL PROGRAM, BY TYPE OF INSTITUTION: 1980–81 AND 1981–82[a]

| | Public Two-Year | | Public Four-Year | | Private Four-Year | | Vocational[b] | | All Institutions | |
|---|---|---|---|---|---|---|---|---|---|---|
| | 1980–81 | 1981–82 | 1980–81 | 1981–82 | 1980–81 | 1981–82 | 1980–81 | 1981–82 | 1980–81 | 1981–82 |
| **Low Income** | | | | | | | | | | |
| Male | 2.0 | 6.6 | 12.3 | 18.1 | 23.9 | 30.5 | 3.9 | 16.7 | 9.5 | 15.6 |
| Female | 1.5 | 2.7 | 4.4 | 9.8 | 10.7 | 22.4 | 5.7 | 6.5 | 4.4 | 9.0 |
| **Moderate Income** | | | | | | | | | | |
| Male | 5.9 | 8.6 | 16.9 | 23.7 | 16.3 | 22.2 | 3.6 | 13.4 | 11.8 | 17.6 |
| Female | 8.3 | 8.9 | 13.3 | 15.3 | 19.3 | 24.0 | 14.7 | 19.1 | 12.7 | 15.0 |
| **High Income** | | | | | | | | | | |
| Male | 6.8 | 8.2 | 16.0 | 14.3 | 31.8 | 32.7 | 4.3 | 9.6 | 16.6 | 16.9 |
| Female | 4.0 | 2.6 | 17.4 | 20.1 | 23.7 | 25.0 | 13.1 | 19.1 | 16.3 | 18.1 |

[a]The base for percentages is all low-income (less than $12,000), moderate-income ($12,000 to $19,000), and high-income ($20,000 and above) 1980 high school seniors enrolled in postsecondary education in 1980–81 and 1981–82.
[b]Category includes all vocational and technical institutions as well as proprietary institutions.

*Source:* U.S. Department of Education 1983.

they had borrowed less, while men wish they had borrowed more.

Women occasionally face discrimination from lenders and a disproportionate burden of repayment for single women (National Commission on Student Financial Assistance 1984). They also face several regulatory restrictions:

1. Eligibility is restricted to students who are attending school at least half time.
2. Veterans' benefits may not be considered in calculating estimated financial assistance, yet other federal grant programs, including AFDC and food stamps, may be.
3. Costs of child care are not explicitly allowed in calculating the cost of attendance.
4. The required written statement from a commercial lender that denies a loan does not have to state the reason for the denial.
5. While schools are required to present prospective students who are likely to obtain a GSL with complete and accurate information about their academic programs, faculty, and facilities, they are not required to provide information of particular concern to women—number of female faculty and administrators, whether or not the campus has child care facilities, and so on (34 CFR 682.200) (Howe, Howard, and Strauss 1982).

*Veterans' benefits may not be considered in calculating estimated financial assistance, yet other federal grant programs, including AFDC and food stamps, may be.*

### Work Study Programs

Women tend to rely more on work study aid than men, but men get the higher-paying jobs. Significant differences are apparent in full-time and part-time college work and summer employment. Greater differences occur in institutionally funded and privately funded work programs than in the federal College Work Study program, except for summer work study (Leslie 1977, 1982; Maxwell 1984; U.S. Department of Education 1983; U.S. Department of Labor 1984).

The College Work Study program, originally part of the Economic Opportunity Act of 1964 and the largest college work program, provides jobs for students. Federal funds pay 80 percent of students' wages in jobs on campus and in nonprofit institutions, thereby providing jobs that would not otherwise exist. College Work Study is popular with institutions because it provides not only student aid but also a pool of subsidized labor. Students may work part time on or off campus; in many instances, they work full time during the summer. Wages, rates, work assignments, supervision, and general management are the responsibility of participating institutions, and, when employment is off campus, work must be in a public or private nonprofit institution. Employment in the program is intended to complement students' educational or vocational goals as much as possible. A total of 3,448 institutions participate in the program; they received approximately $590 million during 1985–86 and provided about 872,660 jobs (U.S. Department of Education 1985a).

*Analysis of participation rates and average awards*
Tabulations on students who rank among the top 20 in their high school graduating class indicate that while the percentage of women participating in College Work Study is higher than that of men (16.5 percent versus 13.8 percent), the average award women receive is less than that of comparable men ($753 versus $830). Further, this award covers less of total college costs than for men (13.7 versus 14.7 percent) (Cooperative Institutional Research Program 1982). Women rely on smaller percentages from total earnings and savings (Cooperative Institutional Research Program 1982; Leslie 1977; National Institute of Independent Colleges and Universities 1983; U.S. Department of Education 1983), and average awards for summer employment differ significantly for men and women (Maxwell 1984). Unemployment among youths is much higher than overall unemployment, and the unemployment rates for blacks and women are even higher. For young black women, the unemployment rate may reach 50 percent (National Student Aid Coalition 1985). Virtually no research on student aid, however, has specifically addressed differences between men and women in average earnings and hourly wage rates.

*Among teenagers, the female-to-male earnings ratio for full-time workers was 87.6 percent—slightly higher than that for 20- to 24-year-olds, and considerably higher than that for other age groups. However, a large number of young workers have earnings at or near the pre-*

*vailing minimum wage ($3.35 per hour in 1982, or $134 for a 40-hour work week). About one-third of the male teenagers and nearly half of the female teenagers earned under $150 a week in 1982* (U.S. Department of Labor 1984, p. 18).

### Policy issues
The requirement for "maintenance of effort" (46 CFR 675.20) provides an opportunity for institutions to increase their own aid programs for women. To meet the requirement, an institution may include any expenditures of its own funds for scholarships, grants, loans, tuition waivers, fee waivers, and fee remissions, and it may include employment of graduate and undergraduate students, whether or not they are eligible for SEOGs or the CWS program. The requirement may also be met by using any funds donated to the institution for financial aid if the institution chooses the recipients and the amounts of awards.

Although students have to show financial need, schools have broad discretion in allocating assistance, and they do not necessarily target it toward the lowest-income students (Penner 1984). Furthermore, no regulatory provisions require equal pay for equal work, one of the most significant policy issues affecting women's participation in student aid, particularly in summer employment. Because the program is being proposed for expansion, it becomes imperative to examine closely the issues of equity (U.S. Department of Education 1983).

### National Direct Student Loans
As an outgrowth of the National Defense Education Act of 1958, which provided student loans for expanding the pool of technologically educated workers in response to the launch of *Sputnik,* NDSLs now provide a "flexible," campus-based source of low-interest loans available to graduate and undergraduate students based on financial need. Because it is the only program that cancels part of the loans for qualifying teachers and extends provisions for repayment for low-income individuals, it is among the most beneficial loan programs for women.

Like other federal student aid programs, funds must be used solely to meet educational and related expenses, and students must be enrolled at least half time at an eligible school. Loans are made from an institution's revolving loan fund, which is comprised of a federal capital contribution, the institution's contribution (10 percent of the federal contribution), and collections from earlier loans. Funds currently are loaned at 5 percent interest to students who have difficulty obtaining other loans or who need additional funds. Distribution of new federal capital is based on state appropriations, regulatory criteria determining an institution's need for funds, and the institution's performance in collecting debts. Federal appropriations for the NDSL program in 1985–86 amounted to over $187 million; 3,250 institutions participated, benefiting an estimated 781,015 students (U.S. Department of Education 1985a).

### Analysis of participation rates and average awards

Students may borrow up to $3,000 for the first two years of an undergraduate program, up to a cumulative maximum of $6,000 for an undergraduate course of study. Graduate students may borrow a maximum of $12,000, minus any amount borrowed as an undergraduate. Average award per recipient, percentage of total costs covered, and percentage of students participating are roughly equal for men and women (Cooperative Institutional Research Program 1982); thus, the program is especially beneficial for women.

Funding for NDSLs has dropped by $107 million since 1980, however, thus serving 100,000 fewer low-income students. Further, funding for the program has been cut off for institutions whose default rate is above 25 percent, many of which are proprietary institutions enrolling the largest proportions of women (U.S. Department of Education 1982). Unfortunately, students sometimes become scapegoats for poor management by a few institutions and consequently are frequently unable to obtain funds from other sources.

*The current practice of eliminating new capital contributions to institutions above the 25 percent benchmark penalizes needy students and not the institutions. New and continuing students who qualify for and need NDSL awards to complete their educations are not the cause of the past default rate problem. Yet they are the ones who will pay the price when institutions are precluded from receiving capital contributions under the program. Con-*

*gress should not permit needy students to be forced to
pay the price for what may have been past institutional
deficiencies regarding collection efforts.**

### Policy issues

The issues of loan burden, default, and bankruptcy have
not been examined with relation to their impact on women.
Default rates for NDSLs are the most prevalent and persis-
tent problem plaguing most participating institutions.
Moreover, women are especially vulnerable to NDSL regulations requiring that students be enrolled at least half
time to receive an NDSL. This requirement impedes the
participation of women, especially at community colleges
and proprietary institutions where women are more likely
to be enrolled less than half time and the institutions are
more likely to deny requests for GSLs.

In the early history of the NDSL program, recipients
could cancel loans for teaching in nearly any type of educational institution, from kindergarten through graduate
school. This policy was rescinded during the 1970s (Moore
1983), however, and as more classroom teachers are
needed, it deserves to be reconsidered.

### Pell Grants

One of the most dramatic revolutions in student financial
assistance was the creation of Basic Educational Opportunity Grants, later renamed Pell Grants after their sponsor,
Senator Claiborne Pell. The idea of such grants was originally greeted with skepticism, antagonism, and resistance
on the part of the higher education community. Senator
Pell, then virtually unknown to education lobbyists,
pushed with commitment and persistence the notion of a
student aid program that would be "direct, basic, and simple," providing students with a "floor" of financial aid to
help defray the costs of postsecondary education (Gladieux
and Wolanin 1976, p. 86). Today it is the largest federal
student grant program based on need, both in terms of dollars appropriated and number of students served.

*Earl Lazerson, president of Southern Illinois University at Edwardsville,
13 August 1982, in correspondence to Alex Lacey, president of Sangamon
State University. Background material for testimony on NDSL defaults
before the Subcommittee on Postsecondary Education, U.S. House of
Representatives.

*Analysis of participation rates and average awards*

An important measure of Pell Grants' effectiveness is the degree to which the award provides a "floor of support" for financing access to postsecondary education. Reflecting their low-income profile, females participate at a higher rate than males (64 percent), but they receive an average award of $880, compared to an average award of $913 for males. The average award tends to be even lower for females in the top 20 of their high school class (Cooperative Institutional Research Program 1982). For both sexes, the award covers only about 16 percent of total costs; thus, the lower average award for females indicates they are attending lower-cost institutions.

The number of low- and moderate-income individuals has declined noticeably since 1980. Females tend to participate at a higher rate in the Pell Grant program (25.5 percent versus 22.8 percent), yet the decreased participation of low-income females (13.3 percent) was about twice that of low-income males (8.5 percent) (U.S. Department of Education 1983). For minority students, the Pell Grant program:

> . . . *seems to have contributed more to increasing access than to increasing choice, since the great majority of recipients are enrolled in lower-cost institutions. Although the awards are higher for students who attend higher-cost institutions, they cover a smaller proportion of the total costs of such schools* (Williams and Kent 1982, p. 36).

*Policy issues*

Current awards are limited to the least of: (1) the maximum award ($1,800) minus the expected family contribution; or (2) one-half of the cost; or (3) the cost minus the expected family contribution. Consequently, some students whose costs are the same but who receive different family contributions receive the same amount. Financial aid administrators do not actually determine eligibility and amounts of Pell Grants; rather, the aid is based on estimates. Thus, the current program results in unintended inequities, as low-income students attending low-cost community colleges are limited to one-half of that low cost; further, the grants generally do not cover costs of transportation or child care.

Certain regulatory policies restrict females' participation in the program:

1. Eligibility is restricted to full-time undergraduate students (34 CFR 690.4).
2. Expenses for child care are not included as an allowable cost of attendance, nor is an adequate amount authorized for miscellaneous expenses. Besides tuition and fees and room and board, allowable costs of attendance include $400 for books, supplies, and miscellaneous expenses for an academic year (34 CFR 690.51).
3. Institutions are in no way required to account for average awards or participation rates on the basis of gender or race (34 CFR 690.85).

**Supplemental Educational Opportunity Grants**
The Supplemental Educational Opportunity Grant (SEOG) program is especially important for students with higher costs of attendance (those attending independent institutions) and of particular concern to women (those who are independent students with dependents). It is often used to recruit top students. The program channels grants to students through institutions, usually as part of a financial aid package, to supplement students' resources when their financial needs are unmet by other sources of aid. During 1985–86, 4,261 institutions received $408 million in SEOG funds, benefiting close to 659,000 students (U.S. Department of Education 1985a). Yet women in some income levels and in the top 20 of their classes receive lower average awards, which cover lower percentages of total college costs, than comparable males (see table 12) (Cooperative Institutional Research Program 1982).

Federal funds are allocated by statutory formula, first to states and then to institutions within the state. Institutions qualify for funds based on past use of funds, current students' finances, and funds allotted to the state where the institution is located. The state allotment is based in part on its relative share of national part-time and full-time undergraduate enrollment (34 CFR 676.3–.6).

A recognized advantage of SEOGs is that they have been able to meet the special circumstances and needs of individual students, and the program has been directed

## TABLE 12
## AVERAGE SUPPLEMENTAL EDUCATIONAL OPPORTUNITY GRANT FOR DEPENDENT FRESHMEN[a]

| | | | Annual Income | | | |
| | 0–$10,000 | $10,000–20,000 | $20,000–30,000 | $30,000–40,000 | $40,000+ | Total |
|---|---|---|---|---|---|---|
| **Male** | | | | | | |
| Average per recipient | $790 | $702 | $750 | $971 | $886 | $755 |
| Percent of cost covered | 15.0 | 13.2 | 14.1 | 14.2 | 13.9 | 13.3 |
| Percent participating | 17.0 | 12.5 | 7.3 | 3.6 | 1.3 | 6.3 |
| **Female** | | | | | | |
| Average per recipient | $787 | $708 | $676 | $743 | $870 | $726 |
| Percent of cost covered | 15.7 | 13.9 | 13.0 | 13.7 | 13.8 | 13.3 |
| Percent participating | 14.5 | 12.3 | 7.1 | 3.4 | 1.3 | 6.5 |

[a]Students in top 20 of class.

*Source:* Cooperative Institutional Research Program 1982.

increasingly at students in high-cost institutions. Because the program is campus based and financial aid officers can design flexible student aid packages, it can be used as an effective tool for recruitment. As a recruiting device, however, SEOGs may be recognizing high-achieving males more than high-achieving females (Cooperative Institutional Research Program 1982).

*Analysis of participation rates and average awards*
The maximum grant authorized per student for a single academic year is $2,000; however, low-income females attending private four-year institutions receive fewer awards than comparable males (24.7 percent versus 35.6 percent of enrollments). Approximately 70 percent of recipients come from families with incomes below $15,000, and over 80 percent also receive Pell Grants. Students at independent institutions received over 40 percent of SEOG funds in 1981–82; only half of Pell Grant recipients in independent institutions and less than 20 percent of Pell Grant recipients in public institutions received a SEOG. Moderate- and high-income females tend to receive equal or slightly higher awards than their male counterparts, although the participation of both low-income males and females has dropped substantially while that of moderate- and high-income students appears to have stabilized (U.S. Department of Education 1983).

*However, low-income females attending private four-year institutions receive fewer awards than comparable males.*

*Policy issues*
To be eligible, a student must be enrolled at least half time and must be an undergraduate. Although an institution may use up to 10 percent of its allocation to award SEOGs to eligible students who are enrolled as less than half-time students, less than 1 percent of participating institutions take advantage of the option. Reporting requirements for the institution cover over 20 pages and do not include any information by gender. Further, if an institution requests a review of the amount of funds it is scheduled to receive, the National Appeal Panel does not consider any items in cost of attendance of concern to women, such as child care (34 CFR 676.7).

Institutions have considerable discretion in selecting recipients of SEOGs. Although federal regulations require that an institution's selection procedures be "uniformly applied, in writing, and maintained in the files of the student financial assistance office'' [34 CFR 676.9 (c) (3)], no available evidence indicates that school officials pay close attention to any issues of gender in selecting recipients.

**State Scholarship and Grant Programs**
Over the past decade, states quadrupled their financial support to postsecondary education, and that support is now an integral part of the total picture (see table 13). The size, type, and impact—as well as the rules governing eligibility—of the programs vary widely from state to state (Davis 1983; Nolfi 1983). In fact, states have consistently provided primary support for all aspects of postsecondary education, increasing from 62.7 percent of total institutional funding in 1970 to 68.5 percent in 1982. State grant programs increased 27 percent since 1980, compared to a 19 percent decrease (in constant dollars) in total federal aid (College Board 1985).

State governors are emerging as powerful leaders in determining the direction of state aid programs, and they have taken a lead in recognizing the financial needs of women (National Governors Association 1985). Former Governor Charles Robb, chair of the National Governors Association's Subcommittee on Education, recommended five policies for states to act on to the 1985 annual conference of governors:

1. Identify and evaluate existing state policies and goals on postsecondary education;
2. Establish more detailed measures of the adequacy of financial aid to evaluate its capacity to ensure that all qualified students have access to postsecondary education and a broad choice of quality institutions;
3. Review and strengthen existing monitoring policies and practices about state financial aid loan authorities;
4. Develop a long-range strategy for improving the allocation of existing financial aid to better serve expected demographic shifts, including more adult, part-time, women, low-income, and minority students;
5. Explore options for restructuring state appropriations to meet projected future demands (National Governors Association 1985, p. 35).

TABLE 13

## AID AWARDED TO POSTSECONDARY STUDENTS IN CONSTANT DOLLARS: 1980–81 THROUGH 1984–85
### (IN MILLIONS)

| | 1980–81 | 1981–82 | Estimated 1982–83 | Estimated 1983–84 | Estimated 1984–85 | Percent Change 1980–81 to 1984–85 |
|---|---|---|---|---|---|---|
| **Federally Supported Programs** | | | | | | |
| **Generally Available Aid** | | | | | | |
| Pell Grants | 2,660 | 2,358 | 2,379 | 2,643 | 2,509 | − 5.7 |
| SEOG | 408 | 371 | 337 | 335 | 338 | − 17.2 |
| SSIG | 85 | 79 | 72 | 57 | 69 | − 18.8 |
| CWS | 734 | 640 | 619 | 664 | 601 | − 18.1 |
| NDSL | 774 | 595 | 585 | 565 | 529 | − 31.7 |
| GSL and PLUS | 6,914 | 7,494 | 6,497 | 7,401 | 7,660 | 10.8 |
| Subtotal | 11,576 | 11,536 | 10,489 | 11,665 | 11,707 | 1.1 |
| **Specially Directed Aid** | | | | | | |
| Social security | 2,099 | 2,047 | 721 | 209 | 32 | − 98.5 |
| Veterans | 1,911 | 1,385 | 1,333 | 1,003 | 757 | − 60.4 |
| Other grants | 132 | 105 | 81 | 57 | 54 | − 59.1 |
| Other loans | 68 | 90 | 155 | 188 | 253 | 272.1 |
| Subtotal | 4,209 | 3,626 | 2,289 | 1,456 | 1,095 | − 74.0 |
| **Total Federal Aid** | 15,785 | 15,162 | 12,778 | 13,122 | 12,802 | − 18.9 |
| **State Grant Programs** | 893 | 944 | 989 | 1,069 | 1,137 | 27.3 |
| **Institutionally Awarded Aid** | 2,383 | 2,382 | 2,384 | 2,384 | 2,384 | 0.0 |
| **Total Federal, State, and Institutional Aid** | 19,062 | 18,489 | 16,151 | 16,575 | 16,323 | − 14.4 |

*Source:* College Board 1985, p. 6.

One significant federal program, State Student Incentive Grants (SSIGs), encourages states to develop their own aid systems for establishing and expanding scholarships. Every federal dollar goes directly to the student, and federal funds are matched with state funds. The program has created a nationwide delivery network of state agencies and officials focusing on student assistance. The largest such network, the National Association of State Scholarship and Grant Programs, is a highly resourceful research, information, and support group for many throughout the financial aid community. A current Department of Education priority for SSIG is to develop and expand state-funded work study programs.* Most states solicit matching corporate dollars, not only for work programs but also for scholarship and grant programs.

Some states—Michigan, New Jersey, Washington, Massachusetts, California, and Oregon—have created special programs for women, and several states recognize women's needs for aid not only in public policy but also by piloting creative initiatives to reduce further financial barriers. Oregon, for example, developed a statewide dissemination system for information on student aid in conjunction with the state's public welfare computer system. Michigan is one of the few states to prohibit explicitly sex discrimination in the distribution of scholarships by statutory language (Michigan Higher Education 1985). The Massachusetts Higher Education Assistance Corporation targets student loan programs for low-income women, in an effort to remove them from public welfare programs. On the other hand, some state officials and agencies have been defendants in bitter court battles to achieve equal opportunity for women.

The SSIG program has been successful; in 1981, for example, at least 26 states matched their increased SSIG funding on about a six-to-one basis (Davis 1983). In addition, SSIG funds contributed to the establishment of new programs in 21 states and to the growth and expansion of programs in seven of those states. Among the 25 states with larger, older programs, SSIG funding has been associated with growth and expansion of programs, and, among

*Terrell H. Bell, 4 May 1983, correspondence to Chancellor John B. Duff, Massachusetts Board of Regents.

five states with older, smaller programs, SSIG funding contributed significantly to programs' growth in three states (Davis 1983). SSIG has been less successful in inducing increased state spending, however (Hansen 1983), largely because federal expenditures fall short of matching many states' efforts. "In fact, declining federal appropriations threaten to erode SSIG's influence on the expansion of state programs altogether. . . . In a time of extreme budgetary pressures on state governments, encouraging the continuation of current spending on state grants might be an important new effect of SSIG" (p. 18).

### Athletic Scholarships

University presidents and athletic coaches have been willing to pay top dollar to recruit winning athletes, expecting the investment to pay off in revenue from television contracts, contributions from alumni, institutional publicity, and general gate receipts. Football and basketball, in particular, generate millions of dollars for several universities. Yet scandals in college sports programs have been mounting, and many of the best National Collegiate Athletic Association (NCAA) universities have been plagued with infractions and scandals involving student aid.

The picture is different for women's sports, which generally fall under "expenditures" in university budgets. Much of the controversy surrounding Title IX regulations has centered on intercollegiate athletics, an area of alleged sex discrimination in higher education as well as the area that provides the largest amounts of student financial assistance. Where men are afforded opportunities for athletic scholarships, women must also be provided similar opportunities. Specifically, "to the extent that a recipient [institution] awards athletic scholarships or grants-in-aid, it must provide reasonable opportunities for such awards for members of each sex in interscholastic or intercollegiate athletics" [34 CFR 106.37 (c)].

The U.S. Department of Education has clarified the obligations of recipients of federal aid under Title IX:

*The Department will examine compliance with this provision of the regulation primarily by means of a financial comparison to determine whether proportionately equal amounts of financial assistance [scholarship aid] are available to men's and women's athletics programs. The*

*Department will measure compliance with this standard by dividing the amounts of aid available for members of each sex by the numbers of male or female participants in the athletics program and comparing results. Institutions may be found in compliance if this comparison results in substantially equal amounts or if a resulting disparity can be explained by adjustments to take into account legitimate, nondiscriminatory factors* (U.S. Department of Education 1979, p. 2).

Various legal actions have been attempted to make Title IX regulations invalid with respect to athletic scholarships and other financial support for student athletes [*NCAA* v. *Califano,* 622 F.2d 1382 (10th Cir. 1980)], although, since the passage of Title IX, no university has been denied federal funds as a consequence of being found negligent by the Office for Civil Rights in the award of athletic scholarships. The university's receipt of a Letter of Finding merely requires remedial actions; nevertheless, an NCAA sanction carries with it not only a loss of scholarships but also the loss of significant revenue as the result of prohibitions against competing in national championships.

Financing collegiate athletics clearly involves some underlying problems pertaining to student financial assistance:

1. Intercollegiate athletics tends to be shrouded in secrecy.
2. Providing equal opportunity for women would require major expenditures for intercollegiate competition and would lead to financial disaster for higher education institutions with NCAA Division I programs.
3. Subsidized athletes, particularly in football and basketball, usually have all tuition, room and board, and living expenses paid by the athletic program.
4. Financial aid is so expensive that relatively few institutions use their full quota of awards and many institutions severely restrict the award per student, providing only partial support to athletes skilled in sports that do not produce revenue.
5. In the NCAA Division I institutions, the typical women's program depends somewhat on the financial success of men's football for budgetary support, although most of the funds for women's programs come from institutional sources rather than gate receipts.

6. Academic scholarships are seldom as numerous or as generous as athletic grants-in-aid.
7. Even though women account for only 30 percent of the total population involved in collegiate athletics, the costs of equalizing their status would be so high that institutions would experience significant budgetary strains, especially private institutions with high tuition costs.
8. Major institutions often provide lucrative and sometimes undemanding summer jobs to recruits as a way to beat the competition, and national rules and enforcement for those jobs may be somewhat looser than enforcement of rules on support during the academic year (Atwell, Grimes, and Lopiano 1980).

Ironically, despite extensive NCAA rules on student aid and Title IX policies requiring sex equity in athletic financial aid, the only way of determining what benefits individual players receive has been to question individual athletes (*Chronicle of Higher Education* 1984).* Power and influence in collegiate athletics are perhaps best illustrated in the 1985 conference schedule of the National Collegiate Athletic Association: The NCAA Women's Round Table met at the same time the NCAA Presidents' Commission was meeting in a closed-door session.

**Military Scholarships and Veterans' Benefits**
Two inadvertent consequences of the GI Bill were the decreased proportion of females enrolled in universities shortly after World War II and a current predominance of males in top executive positions requiring college degrees. The GI Bill, which marked the beginning of the federal role as a provider of student assistance, is recognized as one of the most fitting rewards for national service. Over 17 million individuals have obtained educational benefits under one of the GI bills since World War II, almost all of them male. Based on a fundamental belief that the national interest required large numbers of highly trained individuals, these education assistance programs were designed to help veterans obtain an educational status they might normally

*John Toner, NCAA president, at a press conference during the 1985 NCAA convention, 13 January 1985.

have aspired to and obtained had they not served their country during war or national emergency. A secondary objective was to prevent massive unemployment (Rashkow 1976).

Covering tuition costs and benefits is a top recruiting mechanism for the U.S. armed services. Programs like the veterans' cost-of-instruction payments to institutions of higher education provide funds for veterans' educational needs. Institutions may use this money to "establish and maintain a full-time Office of Veterans' Affairs that provides outreach and recruitment activities, counseling and tutorial services, and special programs for educationally disadvantaged veterans" (34 CFR 629.1). Few women, even though their numbers are increasing, participate in the GI Bill's benefits, however. In 1982, for example, 7.4 percent of women received bachelor's degrees in military sciences, compared to 92.6 percent of men (U.S. Department of Education 1984c).

More options for public service that provide aid for women should be available, and various proposals have suggested an expansion of opportunities for national service by which individuals have a greater choice of ways to serve their country. Most notable is the "GI Bill for Teachers," a proposal to recruit classroom teachers, as more classroom teachers than military personnel are needed over the next 10 years.

### Job Training Financial Aid Programs

Colleges play a vital role in promoting and improving opportunities for careers through job training programs like cooperative education, vocational education, and the Job Training Partnership Act. As salaries and job placements generally are considerably less for women, the financing of job training programs is especially important. Cooperative education, authorized under Title VIII of the Higher Education Act of 1980 and administered by the Office of Vocational and Adult Education in the U.S. Department of Education, has provided over 1,054 grants totaling almost $35 million to postsecondary institutions to develop, implement, strengthen, or expand work programs. These programs contribute to a more direct relationship between college major and full-time employment after graduation. The majority of participating students are compensated for their work; thus, the income is viewed as another form of student financial assistance. Although cooperative education holds considerable potential for improving job skills, national statistics on the participation of women are not collected.

The Carl D. Perkins Vocational Education Act of 1984 (P.L. 98–524), which amends the Vocational Education Act of 1963, attempts to eliminate sex-role stereotyping in occupational training by calling for the reduction of sex biases in vocational education programs. Under the act, interested parties may secure support for projects of national significance to ensure sexual equity based on needs and yearly initiatives of the Office of Vocational and Adult Education. A designated priority is to include programs designed to attract women into nontraditional occupations. Notable accomplishments include awarding credit for previous work, addressing the vocational needs of women offenders, facilitating employment of displaced homemakers, and developing a support service system for sex equity services in vocational education.

The recently enacted Job Training Partnership Act is especially important to women who have lost jobs as a result of industries' closing down. JTPA provided funding to a total of 800,000 people during its first year of operation—48 percent of whom were women—and placed 70 percent of participants. Because state and local governments have great discretion in distributing these funds, however, it is not known how women fare compared to men in terms of actual amount of money received.

# IMPLICATIONS FOR INSTITUTIONAL PRACTICES

While individuals in Congress, in federal agencies, and in the higher education community have spent significant amounts of energy, time, and money to improve financial aid, the ultimate factor that determines whether or not a student receives adequate financial resources is the commitment, leadership, and knowledge of university officials. Regardless of what Congress may enact, all is lost when personnel in a student aid office do not know of laws or—worse yet—do not care. And federal regulations for Title IV programs of the Higher Education Act give institutions considerable discretion over the administration of student aid programs, particularly the campus-based College Work Study, SEOG, and NDSL programs.

*All is lost when personnel in a student aid office do not know of laws or—worse yet—do not care.*

Institutional policies establish the manner and the extent to which federal and nonfederal aid programs can be used on campus. Universities, for example, may administer fellowships and assistantships for women to comply with the maintenance-of-effort requirements of the College Work Study program. GSL regulations require institutions to provide adequate information about curriculum, faculty, and so on in their recruiting students. The extent to which this information includes items of particular concern to women—the number of women on the faculty and in administrative positions, whether the campus provides child care, or policies ensuring fairness to women—is completely at the discretion of the institution (Bogart, Flagle, and Jung 1974; Howe, Howard, and Strauss 1982). Federal regulations do not require an institution to target its information toward women or minorities, and a review of the 1985 list of federally approved accreditation agencies shows virtually no provisions to examine student aid practices on campus.

Improving students' access to information and women's access to financial aid requires first an examination of policies and procedures related to partnerships between secondary and postsecondary institutions, institutional self-assessments, student financial support services, practices of financial aid offices, partnerships with the private sector, and institutional leadership.

## Administrative Leadership

The level of commitment to equitable assistance for women varies widely from campus to campus, depending on the interest of the president and the trustees. Leadership from college presidents, university administrators, and boards of trustees is essential if student aid is to be divided equitably. University boards of trustees in particular can play a more useful role in shaping practices by restructuring committee systems and reemphasizing the board's role in evaluating policy. Female members on boards of trustees are an especially valuable resource for making sure female students are provided with adequate financial support. Senior officials should consistently and explicitly express commitment to equalizing student aid for men and women, best expressed in annual reports, statements of policy and procedure, guidelines for recruitment, and public addresses. The essential test of educational policy, simply put, is whether or not individuals are afforded every opportunity to achieve their maximum academic, economic, and personal potential.

**Improving Partnerships between Schools and Colleges**
Postsecondary institutions are inevitably connected to high schools, high schools inevitably connected to colleges. While recent national attention has focused on such partnerships, little has been done to institutionalize a two-way flow of information about student aid. It is rare to see a college president attend a national conference of the American Association of School Administrators, the major organization representing school superintendents, or to see a superintendent participate in meetings of the American Council on Education, the major organization representing university presidents and other college administrators. Virtually no college recruitment booths can be found among AASA exhibits, while recruitment booths from all four branches of the U.S. armed services are quite extensive. And while the National School Boards Association, one of the most powerful groups influencing the policy of local school districts, sets forth numerous resolutions on issues like "state and local financing of education," "the federal role in education," "programs urging multiagency action," and "state and local policies and programs," it makes no mention of student financial aid (National School Boards Association 1986).

Leadership from school superintendents, school board members, and university presidents is essential in disseminating information about student aid and targeting the information to those low-income students who would not think of attending college because of their financial situation. To receive student aid, a student must first *apply,* and school district officials are in pivotal positions to assist with that process. Thus, district administrators must become more knowledgeable about aid programs and ways to target that information.

Groups like the National Association of Secondary School Principals, the National School Boards Association, and others should announce meeting dates, research findings, and new publications on student aid by the higher education community to their members. Similarly, higher education officials need to keep abreast of economic concerns facing high school students. This flow of information is vital in achieving equal educational opportunity.

**Equal Pay in College Work Programs**
Improving the balance in student aid programs necessitates a review of pay schedules, practices, and benefits in college work programs for both undergraduates and graduates. Because women continue to confront inequitable pay schedules, opportunities for promotions, and benefits, a good starting point for correcting differences is postsecondary institutions. It is difficult to imagine that the job environment will improve for women until graduate teaching assistants are paid the same as research assistants and until off-campus work sites provide more comparable salaries.

Issues of concern involving pay include the distribution of men and women in part-time and full-time jobs, salaries and benefits during summer employment, and type of work on and off campus. Because women attend school primarily to acquire new job skills or to advance in a current job, a logical place to learn practical as well as theoretical skills is on campus. Job information and recruiting services should be reviewed to determine whether they encourage women to obtain jobs in school and upon graduation that relate to their interests and promote equal salaries and job opportunities.

Although the days are gone when students could work their way through college without much additional financial stress, the variations of work study need to be reexamined. Ironically, this program is one of the most important for women attending school, yet it also is where they confront significant problems—lack of information on summer employment, unequal pay, and priorities given to full-time students, even when federal allowances are made for part-time students. College work programs—cooperative education, College Work Study, state work programs, the Job Training Partnership, and off-campus employment—are good starting points for women to obtain positive experiences in the workplace.

### Coordination with Public Assistance Offices

While the feminization of poverty affects women of all income groups, it is particularly acute for those who receive public welfare. Very few—if any—welfare offices have information about student aid or college brochures available in waiting rooms or near waiting lines. Further, a coordinated review is necessary of conflicting regulatory policies among public welfare and public housing programs and opportunities for student aid. Perhaps an examination of the issues could use a statutory mechanism already in place, the Federal Interagency Committee on Education.

A recent study recommends six basic strategies for resolving the Catch-22 situation between AFDC programs and student aid rules:

1. Develop effective communication with agencies administering AFDC programs;
2. Assist recipients of AFDC in negotiations for job searches, work, and other requirements that can conflict with enrollment in postsecondary education;
3. Influence the way student financial aid is treated in the calculation of income and resources;
4. Assist recipients of AFDC to secure child care;
5. Help recipients of AFDC understand the complexities of student financial aid and AFDC programs, including their rights and responsibilities as recipients;
6. Stay abreast of regulations and administrative procedures in the AFDC program that might affect the way recipients enrolled in postsecondary education are treated (Hansen and Franklin 1984).

**Provisions for Child Care**

Improving the provision of child care is one of the greatest challenges for postsecondary institutions (Project on the Status and Education of Women 1980). A review of provisions should include the percentage of requests met and the extent of state and local supplements. The data bank on child care systems should be expanded. A woman's ability to participate in class many times depends on the availability of immediate child care. Institutions have a responsibility to provide information about the type of services available, which should include information about services in the community as well as on-campus facilities, and that information should be provided up front, in tables of contents of university catalogs and on campus maps. Credit for working in child care centers should be provided for university students interested in early childhood education.

**Outreach**

Improving the dissemination of information is a critical step toward improving women's participation in student aid programs. Nontraditional students in particular should be targeted. Universities have at least an ethical obligation to provide sufficient information about student aid and assistance with applications to those who receive public welfare and unemployment benefits and to displaced homemakers. Exemplary outreach programs should include special scholarship programs for women, options for forgiving some or all of a loan, on-campus banking and financial counseling, student credit unions chartered by the National Credit Union, and news about financial aid published regularly in student newspapers. Other areas that could be improved include fund raising for endowments, the availability of weekend degree programs, and public service radio and television announcements.

All campus publications—campus maps, class schedules, university catalogs—need to be reviewed from the perspective of whether or not they provide as much information about student aid as possible. Workshops and informational seminars are especially worthwhile as students apply to graduate school or law school; they should include individualized assistance and information about applying for student aid, international internships, merit scholarships, and available college work programs.

### Transfer Students
Because women are more likely to be transfer students—either from community colleges or because of a husband's job-related move—their costs of education are likely to be higher. Often, credits from the previous institution are not accepted, requiring coursework to be repeated. A related issue is that student aid, particularly campus-based programs and institutionally awarded scholarships, generally is not transferable.

### Nondegree, Unclassified, and Remedial Coursework
Women are more likely than men to take courses to satisfy their own interest or desire for knowledge, to upgrade job skills, or simply to develop confidence to undertake a degree program. Although financial assistance generally is not available for such courses, some notable programs to assist these students frequently take the form of reduced charges for tuition. At Southern Illinois University–Edwardsville, for example, anyone not enrolled in courses for credit may attend selected classes under the "EDU-CARD" program as space is available for a fee of $15.

On the other hand, women are also more likely to enroll in remedial courses because they are the victim of biases against girls' taking math and science courses in elementary and secondary schools. In the climate of improving educational excellence, the notion of granting credit toward a degree for remedial coursework—or even providing remedial coursework at the university level—is increasingly controversial. Yet some kind of credit is necessary to enable students to qualify for student financial aid, because most student aid is based upon credit hours taken. Many times a remedial course can be the determining factor in whether a student is considered full time or part time, with full-time students generally eligible to receive larger amounts of aid. University officials need to be careful in reviewing policies regarding credit for remedial coursework. Sometimes nondegree credit can be given to assist in a student's qualifying for financial aid. Classes can then be figured in a student's courseload but not applied toward a degree program.

**Student Aid from the Private Sector**
Given the reality of severe deficits in the federal budget,
financial constraints on institutions and states, and reduced
federal support for postsecondary education, one untapped
source of financial assistance for students is the private
sector (Moran 1983). School district officials, having more
discretion with private scholarships and being able to snip
the red tape associated with applications, can quickly target money for low-income students, especially those who
are not applying to college or talking about college. Money
can be easily targeted to high schools with disproportionately high dropout rates—those on Indian reservations, in
rural farm areas, and in inner city ghettos.

Sources of private student aid are virtually unlimited
(Johnson and Smith 1984; Renz 1985; Schlachter 1982), but
the systematic solicitation and targeting of funds must be
improved. While major sources currently include individual
philanthropy, corporate scholarships, trust funds, and college
endowment funds, other emerging trends deserve attention,
in particular the trend of congressional and presidential candidates' setting up tax-exempt foundations as a way to
receive almost unlimited individual and corporate contributions for noncampaign purposes, thereby bypassing requirements for financial reporting of the Federal Election Commission. One model example is the Dole Foundation for
Employment of Persons with Disabilities, established by Senator Robert Dole to provide money to nonprofit programs to
help the disabled find training and jobs. In one evening fun-
draiser alone, the foundation received over $1 million.
Another example is Washington's farewell tribute to retiring
House Speaker Thomas P. O'Neill, in which one dinner
raised over $1 million in scholarship aid for Boston College,
O'Neill's alma mater. Women are themselves generally in
positions to set up scholarship funds, as they frequently outlive their husbands.

**Review of Accrediting Agencies**
One of the most powerful agents for improving and changing institutional practices is the accreditation agency, yet
virtually no accrediting group pays close attention to the
distribution, impact, or amount of financial assistance for
students in any given program. The U.S. Department of
Education recognizes over 100 accreditation agencies,

among them the American Bar Association, the North Central Association of Colleges and Schools, the American Library Association, the American Optometric Association, the American Medical Association, the National Council on Accreditation for Teacher Education, and state agencies like the Arkansas State Board for Vocational Education, the Montana State Board of Nursing, and the Oklahoma State Regents for Higher Education.

A typical accreditation review team is comprised of a management specialist, an educational specialist, a subject-matter specialist for each curriculum area, and a representative of the accrediting agency. Although postsecondary institutions must be accredited by a recognized accrediting group to be eligible to receive federal student aid, accrediting groups generally do not consider student aid as a factor in accreditation. And no institution has ever been denied accreditation for not providing and ensuring women's educational equity.

Administrators of accreditation agencies need to seek out student aid experts to participate on evaluation teams, to provide consulting services for the evaluation and accreditation process, and to serve on policy-making boards. Moreover, an institution's commitment to educational equity for women needs increased emphasis in required, ongoing program evaluations. And having more individuals who are expert in student aid on the Federal Advisory Committee on Accreditation and Institutional Eligibility would be beneficial.

**Loan Forgiveness**
Women are most at risk for defaulting on a loan and declaring bankruptcy. They may be the primary applicants for loan consolidation, particularly as women's salaries are notoriously low upon graduation from college. Loan repayment burdens in all major loan programs can be better curtailed by implementing repayment plans contingent upon income and loan forgiveness options rather than through the administratively complex and costly system of consolidation. A plan similar to the IRS's system for withholding payments on borrowers who default can be set up by automatically adjusting payments on the basis of an individual's annual adjusted gross income. Using such a nationally uniform computer system would increase cost effectiveness.

Options for loan forgiveness can readily be established through universities, employers, government agencies, school districts, and hospitals. A model example is the program for teaching in targeted areas, established through the NDSL program, and of particular merit is the implementation of a "GI Bill for Teachers" advocated by the American Federation of Teachers. More teachers are needed in the next few years; thus, expanding the available options for forgiving loans is a viable strategy for recruiting teachers and also for reducing women's burden of debt. For example, 69 percent of nursing students could not continue nursing school without financial assistance, and 67 percent have said they would be willing to work in an underserved, low-income area in return for having part of a federal loan forgiven (National Student Nurses Association 1985).

Consolidating and refinancing loans present a financial windfall for lending institutions and secondary markets rather than contribute to the relief of individual borrowers. Consolidation would decrease a borrower's monthly payments but extend the repayment period of the loan, usually up to 20 years rather than a maximum of 10 years under current GSL and NDSL regulations. Because women rely more on NDSLs than on GSLs, however, they tend to pay higher interest rates under the most recent Sallie Mae consolidation program.[2] That is, by weighted averaging of interest rates to 7 percent, borrowers who consolidate NDSLs made at 3, 4, or 5 percent experience an increase in interest rates, while those who consolidate a 9 percent GSL experience a decrease. Although the monthly payment would decrease for individual borrowers, the projected costs to the federal government would increase significantly, including the $50 minimum payment to original lenders, increased special allowance, and allowances for administrative costs. According to the U.S. General Accounting Office, the increase on a consolidated loan volume of $100 million would be about $300,000 (about 4 percent) in the first year and about $2.9 million (about 5 percent) over the life of the loans. The debate during exten-

2. Sallie Mae (Student Loan Marketing Association) is a federally chartered, stockholder-owned corporation that provides the nation's largest single source of financing for postsecondary education credit. It offers a variety of financial services to all segments of the education credit market and has provided loan consolidation.

sive congressional hearings on loan consolidation has narrowly centered on whether consolidation should be administered by state guarantee agencies or by the national secondary market (Sallie Mae). No information has been presented, nor is any available, as to *who* has been applying to Sallie Mae's Options program. In fact, it is unknown how many students qualify for loan consolidation (U.S. Congress 1984b, p. 33).

**Corporate Benefit Programs That Pay Tuition**
Immediate attention should address the needs for education and staff development of the growing number of working women, a significant portion of them mothers working full time and regular hours. More research and recruitment are needed to improve the participation of women in corporate programs paying tuition benefits. Partnerships between corporations and universities could include direct billings to the corporation, an increase in on-site training programs, the provision of child care whether an individual is at school or at work, and an expansion of public service instructional television programs.

Corporation managers need to improve the systematic dissemination of information about available programs that pay tuition and should release annual reports of the participation of males and females in the programs as well as their average costs. The income tax deduction for education expenses should also include expenses for child care.

**Title IX Self-Assessment**
One constructive outgrowth of Title IX was the development of guides for institutional self-assessment (Bogart 1981; Caliendo and Curtice 1977; Mathews and McCune 1974). Besides being a diagnostic tool for identifying and eliminating barriers to sexual equity, a guide functions as a data base containing specific trend analyses about the condition, policies, and practices of an institution. As a development tool, a guide can stimulate discussion and familiarize faculty, staff, and students with aspects of their own behavior and the behavior of others that may subtly and unintentionally present barriers against women (Bogart, Flagle, and Jung 1974). As a consequence of such guides, most universities have improved their commitment to equal educational opportunity for women.

Self-assessment guides are not without their problems, however.

*A self-assessment guide, no matter how well intended, inclusive, systematic, or in-depth, cannot assure that sex discrimination is eliminated from policies and practices found in those offices responsible for disseminating campus-based student aid programs. The document can only guide institutions toward points of awareness of real or potential acts of discrimination, no matter how unintentional. The attitude of those responsible for self-evaluation efforts is of the greatest importance. The law and the attendant regulations are shrouded with ambiguities in intent and interpretation. It is easy to gloss over the requirement to search out policies and practices [that] may be discriminatory. Administrators responsible for self-evaluation efforts as well as administrators of programs to be assessed must, in good faith, enter into this key initial task with sincere intentions and with a receptivity to the principle at stake* (Caliendo and Curtice 1977, p. 35).

Ironically, Title IX occasionally exposes a new and complex version of discrimination—that of passive resistance and official decisions made on non-sex-discriminatory bases rather than outright blockage of women's educational ascent (Sandler 1986). Some university administrators have become sophisticated at hiding discriminatory practices, even in civil rights assurances filed with federal agencies for funding. Although postsecondary institutions frequently have Title IX coordinators on their staffs, such individuals generally have no background in student aid, are not involved in mainstream decision making, and generally do not report directly to the president. Consequently, compliance with Title IX frequently means reluctantly submitting to the letter of the law and ignoring the spirit of Title IX. Virtually no Title IX coordinator reports issues related to student aid. And Title IX reports are generally classified as "confidential."

*Grove City* v. *Bell* appears also to be a sophisticated case, permitting continuation of discriminatory practices in some colleges by applying legal logic to peripheral issues like whether or not student aid should be considered as federal aid to the institution. The issue of possible discriminatory practices by plaintiff universities is not mentioned in court briefs when, in fact, evidence suggests that the very universities involved in federal litigation are far below national averages in percentages of women represented on the faculty and in administrative positions. Legal briefs filed in federal courts not only do not describe the distribution of student aid on the basis of sex within the universities involved; they also do not mention any progress in sexual equity that might have been made in admissions, faculty appointments, or women administrators. Substantial evidence suggests that the very universities that are plaintiffs in federal courts arguing that they do not have to comply with Title IX are no models of excellence for educational equity (U.S. Department of Education 1984e). The issue of student aid needs to be examined closely. When asked about the distribution of Pell Grants by gender among Grove City students, for example, the attorney representing the university before the U.S. Supreme Court during oral arguments replied, "There is . . . nothing in the record [that] indicates the proportion by which those students were divided, whether by sex, by minority, by race, by religion, [or] by anything else" (U.S. Supreme Court 1983, p. 11).

# CONCLUSION

## Resources for Research and Information

An unfortunate obstacle to providing needed student aid
for women is the insufficient (generally nonexistent), noncomparable data that can be used to improve policies and
programs. Typically, data collected by the federal government, higher education associations, and institutional student aid offices include no information broken down by
gender. And of over 100 computerized databases containing a wide variety of information on student aid in place
throughout the U.S. Department of Education or under
contract, virtually none include information on gender.

Postsecondary institutions themselves have extensive
technological capacity for collecting, storing, merging, and
retrieving a wide range of information on student finances.
With increasingly sophisticated computer technology, campus systems now can link all departments throughout the
university as well as outside agencies like the College
Scholarship Service, loan collection agencies, the Pell
Grant processing center, and state higher education executive officers.

Issues of equity at all levels of postsecondary education
require ongoing reviews, yet detailed information on the
distribution of aid by gender is severely lacking. Because
applications for student aid do not request information on
gender or race, policy makers have great difficulty assess-
ing whether dollars are indeed reaching minorities and
women as Congress intended. Compounding the problem,
major research efforts to assess the economic concerns of
students have ignored issues of gender (Butler-Nalin,
Sanderson, and Redman 1983; Flamer, Horch, and
Davis 1982).

*An ultimate issue . . . is simply the extent to which women participate substantively in decision making and hold positions of leadership invested with authority and responsibility.*

## The Balance of Power

An ultimate issue determining the impact of student aid
policy on women is simply the extent to which women participate substantively in decision making and hold positions
of leadership invested with authority and responsibility.
The development of federal policy for student aid is an
elaborate and multifacet maze involving congressional
committees, the Council of Economic Advisors, several
offices throughout the U.S. Department of Education, state
guarantee agencies, Sallie Mae, the Office of Management
and Budget, the U.S. Treasury, the Internal Revenue Ser-

vice, the Federal Reserve, and national higher education organizations, among many others. The decision-making processes within these powerful institutions include few women, if any. Student aid formulas, available funds, criteria for eligibility, and application procedures tend to change each year as new economic, political, and educational forces struggle for control of student aid policy. And each year, major changes have been made without the recognition of potential adverse effects on women.

An overlooked—but perhaps most important—recommendation of the National Commission on Excellence in Education was to stress "the distinction between leadership skills involving persuasion, setting goals and developing community consensus behind them, and managerial and supervisory skills." Although managerial and supervisory skills are necessary, it is important to consciously develop persuasive leadership skills if reforms are to be successful. Persuasive leadership requires a commanding understanding of and proficiency in fundamental organization skills—networking, negotiating, building teams and coalitions, risk taking, and developing group processes. At the same time, effective use of these skills depends on a high degree of knowledge of and commitment to a particular cause.

# APPENDIX A

**PERCENTAGE INCREASES IN COLLEGE REVENUES: FY 1979–FY 1982**

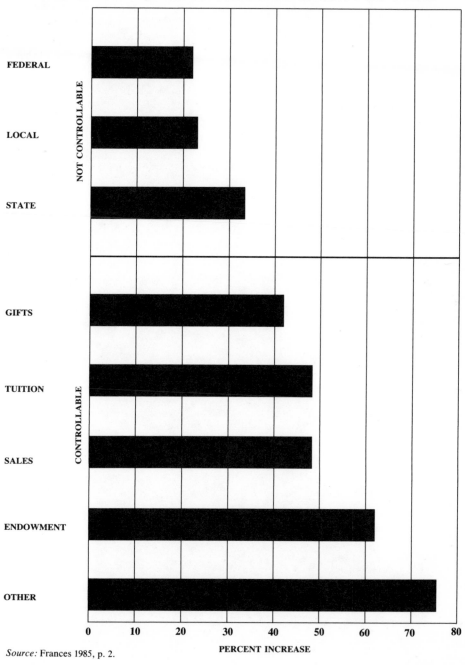

*Source:* Frances 1985, p. 2.

## A-2
## COLLEGE ENROLLMENT BY SEX, AGE, AND RACE: 1970–1982
### (IN THOUSANDS, EXCEPT PERCENT)

| | 1970 | 1972 | 1974 | 1975 | 1976 | 1977 | 1978 | 1979 | 1980 | 1981 | 1982 | Percent 1970 | Percent 1975 | Percent 1982 |
|---|---|---|---|---|---|---|---|---|---|---|---|---|---|---|
| **Total** | 7,327 | 9,095 | 9,851 | 10,880 | 11,139 | 11,546 | 11,140 | 11,380 | 11,387 | 12,127 | 12,309 | 100.0 | 100.0 | 100.0 |
| **Male** | 4,292 | 5,218 | 5,402 | 5,911 | 5,785 | 5,889 | 5,581 | 5,480 | 5,430 | 5,825 | 5,899 | 58.6 | 54.3 | 47.9 |
| 16–24 years | 3,113 | 3,534 | 3,411 | 3,693 | 3,673 | 3,712 | 3,621 | 3,508 | 3,604 | 3,833 | 3,837 | 42.8 | 33.9 | 31.2 |
| 25–34 years | 955 | 1,178 | 1,371 | 1,521 | 1,518 | 1,546 | 1,396 | 1,356 | 1,325 | 1,442 | 1,460 | 13.0 | 14.0 | 11.9 |
| 35 years and over | 178 | 365 | 476 | 569 | 489 | 520 | 457 | 487 | 405 | 453 | 490 | 2.4 | 5.2 | 4.0 |
| **Female** | 3,035 | 3,877 | 4,449 | 4,969 | 5,354 | 5,657 | 5,559 | 5,900 | 5,957 | 6,303 | 6,410 | 41.4 | 45.7 | 52.1 |
| 16–24 years | 2,392 | 2,724 | 2,905 | 3,243 | 3,508 | 3,431 | 3,373 | 3,482 | 3,625 | 3,741 | 3,841 | 32.6 | 29.8 | 31.2 |
| 25–34 years | 430 | 581 | 831 | 947 | 971 | 1,255 | 1,173 | 1,319 | 1,378 | 1,485 | 1,528 | 5.9 | 8.7 | 12.4 |
| 35 years and over | 183 | 418 | 548 | 614 | 700 | 809 | 845 | 914 | 802 | 940 | 900 | 2.5 | 5.6 | 7.3 |
| **White** | 6,721 | 8,147 | 8,689 | 9,547 | 9,679 | 9,961 | 9,662 | 9,956 | 9,926 | 10,352 | 10,550 | 91.7 | 87.7 | 85.7 |
| Male | 3,987 | 4,723 | 4,781 | 5,263 | 5,085 | 5,156 | 4,913 | 4,823 | 4,804 | 5,011 | 5,078 | 54.4 | 48.4 | 41.3 |
| Female | 2,734 | 3,427 | 3,906 | 4,285 | 4,594 | 4,806 | 4,748 | 5,132 | 5,123 | 5,342 | 5,474 | 37.3 | 39.4 | 44.5 |
| **Black and Other Races** | 606 | 949 | 1,163 | 1,333 | 1,460 | 1,585 | 1,479 | 1,424 | 1,461 | 1,775 | 1,758 | 8.3 | 12.3 | 14.3 |
| Male | 305 | 496 | 621 | 648 | 700 | 733 | 668 | 657 | 626 | 814 | 821 | 4.2 | 6.0 | 6.7 |
| Female | 301 | 450 | 543 | 684 | 760 | 851 | 811 | 768 | 834 | 961 | 936 | 4.1 | 6.3 | 7.6 |

While it is difficult to draw statistical conclusions relative to these data that could capture the numerous variables affecting the increase in college enrollment during this 12-year period, some assumptions can be made. The establishment of the State Student Incentive Grants program in 1972 and the Basic Educational Opportunity Grant program (renamed Pell Grant in 1980), awarded in 1973–74, may account in part for the marked increase in enrollment from 1970 to 1972 and 1974. Further, population is projected to increase by 9.7 percent between 1980 and 1990 and by 7.3 percent between 1990 and 2000. This increase will directly affect college enrollment and hence the need for student aid.

*Source:* National Association of Student Financial Aid Administrators 1985a, p. 12.

## A-3
## ENROLLMENT IN INSTITUTIONS OF HIGHER EDUCATION, BY CONTROL AND TYPE OF INSTITUTION AND SEX OF STUDENT: 50 STATES AND D.C., FALL 1979 TO FALL 1982

| | Fall 1979 | Fall 1980 | Fall 1981 | Fall 1982 | Percent Change | | |
|---|---|---|---|---|---|---|---|
| | | | | | 1979–80 | 1980–81 | 1981–82 |
| **Total, All Institutions** | 11,569,899 | 12,096,895 | 12,371,672 | 12,425,780 | +4.6 | +2.3 | +0.4 |
| Doctoral | 2,962,756 | 3,028,868 | 3,046,363 | 3,028,176 | +2.2 | +0.6 | −0.6 |
| Comprehensive | 2,746,604 | 2,813,735 | 2,839,524 | 2,837,745 | +2.4 | +0.9 | −0.1 |
| General baccalaureate | 1,121,749 | 1,172,667 | 1,185,922 | 1,181,015 | +4.5 | +1.1 | −0.4 |
| Specialized | 492,164 | 543,277 | 559,458 | 575,443 | +10.4 | +3.0 | +2.9 |
| Two-year | 4,246,232 | 4,472,085 | 4,630,108 | 4,665,939 | +5.3 | +3.5 | +0.8 |
| New | 394 | 66,263 | 110,297 | 137,462 | +16,718.0 | +66.5 | +24.6 |
| | | | | | | | |
| Men | 5,682,877 | 5,874,374 | 5,975,056 | 6,031,384 | +3.4 | +1.7 | +0.9 |
| Women | 5,887,022 | 6,222,521 | 6,396,616 | 6,394,396 | +5.7 | +2.8 | +0.0 |
| | | | | | | | |
| **Public, Total** | 9,036,822 | 9,457,394 | 9,647,032 | 9,696,087 | +4.7 | +2.0 | +0.5 |
| Men | 4,368,979 | 4,522,587 | 4,586,800 | 4,632,888 | +3.5 | +1.4 | +1.0 |
| Women | 4,667,843 | 4,934,807 | 5,060,232 | 5,063,199 | +5.7 | +2.5 | +0.1 |
| | | | | | | | |
| Doctoral | 2,304,514 | 2,363,946 | 2,367,447 | 2,366,260 | +2.6 | +0.1 | −0.1 |
| Men | 1,222,815 | 1,243,418 | 1,239,295 | 1,243,031 | +1.7 | −0.3 | +0.3 |
| Women | 1,081,699 | 1,120,528 | 1,128,152 | 1,123,229 | +3.6 | +0.7 | −0.4 |
| Comprehensive | 2,147,468 | 2,207,559 | 2,227,725 | 2,224,856 | +2.8 | +0.9 | −0.1 |
| Men | 1,011,261 | 1,030,644 | 1,038,156 | 1,046,402 | +1.9 | +0.7 | +0.8 |
| Women | 1,136,207 | 1,176,915 | 1,189,569 | 1,178,454 | +3.6 | +1.1 | −0.9 |
| General baccalaureate | 375,396 | 395,330 | 401,857 | 410,084 | +5.3 | +1.7 | +2.0 |
| Men | 180,256 | 186,426 | 189,478 | 194,974 | +3.4 | +1.6 | +2.9 |
| Women | 195,140 | 208,904 | 212,379 | 215,110 | +7.1 | +1.7 | +1.3 |
| Specialized | 143,817 | 180,029 | 185,948 | 193,443 | +25.2 | +3.3 | +4.0 |
| Men | 92,287 | 122,951 | 126,647 | 131,747 | +33.2 | +3.0 | +4.0 |
| Women | 51,530 | 57,078 | 59,301 | 61,696 | +10.8 | +3.9 | +4.0 |
| Two-year | 4,065,627 | 4,283,678 | 4,432,157 | 4,463,945 | +5.4 | +3.5 | +0.7 |
| Men | 1,862,360 | 1,926,270 | 1,977,758 | 1,998,341 | +3.4 | +2.7 | +1.0 |
| Women | 2,203,267 | 2,357,408 | 2,454,399 | 2,465,604 | +7.0 | +4.1 | +0.5 |
| New | 0 | 26,852 | 31,898 | 37,499 | +0.0 | +18.8 | +17.6 |
| Men | 0 | 12,878 | 15,466 | 18,393 | +0.0 | +20.1 | +18.9 |
| Women | 0 | 13,974 | 16,432 | 19,106 | +0.0 | +17.6 | +16.3 |

| | | | | | | | |
|---|---|---|---|---|---|---|---|
| **Private, Total** | 2,533,077 | 2,639,501 | 2,724,640 | 2,729,693 | +4.2 | +3.2 | +0.2 |
| Men | 1,313,898 | 1,351,787 | 1,388,256 | 1,398,496 | +2.9 | +2.7 | +0.7 |
| Women | 1,219,179 | 1,287,714 | 1,336,384 | 1,331,197 | +5.6 | +3.8 | −0.4 |
| Doctoral | 658,242 | 664,922 | 678,916 | 661,916 | +1.0 | +2.1 | −2.5 |
| Men | 374,726 | 376,568 | 379,718 | 369,515 | +0.5 | +0.8 | −2.7 |
| Women | 283,516 | 288,354 | 299,198 | 292,401 | +1.7 | +3.8 | −2.3 |
| Comprehensive | 599,136 | 606,176 | 611,799 | 612,889 | +1.2 | +0.9 | +0.2 |
| Men | 315,103 | 313,303 | 312,309 | 312,388 | −0.6 | −0.3 | +0.0 |
| Women | 284,033 | 292,873 | 299,490 | 300,501 | +3.1 | +2.3 | +0.3 |
| General baccalaureate | 746,353 | 777,337 | 784,065 | 770,931 | +4.2 | +0.9 | −1.7 |
| Men | 338,278 | 345,001 | 347,100 | 340,989 | +2.0 | +0.6 | −1.8 |
| Women | 408,075 | 432,336 | 436,965 | 429,942 | +5.9 | +1.1 | −1.6 |
| Specialized | 348,347 | 363,248 | 373,510 | 382,000 | +4.3 | +2.8 | +2.3 |
| Men | 212,408 | 216,355 | 219,353 | 221,853 | +1.9 | +1.4 | +1.1 |
| Women | 135,939 | 146,893 | 154,157 | 160,147 | +8.1 | +4.9 | +3.9 |
| Two-year | 180,605 | 188,407 | 197,951 | 201,994 | +4.3 | +5.1 | +2.0 |
| Men | 73,089 | 73,531 | 77,062 | 80,016 | +0.6 | +4.8 | +3.8 |
| Women | 107,516 | 114,876 | 120,889 | 121,978 | +6.8 | +5.2 | +0.9 |
| New | 394 | 39,411 | 78,399 | 99,963 | +9,902.8 | +98.9 | +27.5 |
| Men | 294 | 27,029 | 52,714 | 73,735 | +9,093.5 | +95.0 | +39.9 |
| Women | 100 | 12,382 | 25,685 | 26,228 | +12,282.0 | +107.4 | +2.1 |

A-3 *(continued)*

ENROLLMENT IN INSTITUTIONS OF HIGHER EDUCATION, BY CONTROL AND TYPE OF INSTITUTION AND SEX OF STUDENT: 50 STATES AND D.C., FALL 1979 TO FALL 1982

| | Fall 1979 | Fall 1980 | Fall 1981 | Fall 1982 | Percent Change | | |
| --- | --- | --- | --- | --- | --- | --- | --- |
| | | | | | *1979–80* | *1980–81* | *1981–82* |
| **Private, Nonprofit** | 2,461,773 | 2,527,787 | 2,572,405 | 2,552,739 | + 2.7 | + 1.8 | − 0.8 |
| Men | 1,281,688 | 1,295,652 | 1,305,426 | 1,292,027 | + 1.1 | + 0.8 | − 1.0 |
| Women | 1,180,085 | 1,232,135 | 1,266,979 | 1,260,712 | + 4.4 | + 2.8 | − 0.5 |
| Doctoral | 658,242 | 664,922 | 678,916 | 661,916 | + 1.0 | + 2.1 | − 2.5 |
| Men | 374,726 | 376,568 | 379,718 | 369,515 | + 0.5 | + 0.8 | − 2.7 |
| Women | 283,516 | 288,354 | 299,198 | 292,401 | + 1.7 | + 3.8 | − 2.3 |
| Comprehensive | 599,136 | 606,176 | 611,799 | 612,889 | + 1.2 | + 0.9 | + 0.2 |
| Men | 315,103 | 313,303 | 312,309 | 312,388 | − 0.6 | − 0.3 | + 0.0 |
| Women | 284,033 | 292,873 | 299,490 | 300,501 | + 3.1 | + 2.3 | + 0.3 |
| General baccalaureate | 741,295 | 772,214 | 778,910 | 766,108 | + 4.2 | + 0.9 | − 1.6 |
| Men | 335,942 | 342,706 | 344,781 | 338,840 | + 2.0 | + 0.6 | − 1.7 |
| Women | 405,353 | 429,508 | 434,129 | 427,268 | + 6.0 | + 1.1 | − 1.6 |
| Specialized | 334,802 | 344,958 | 352,404 | 359,334 | + 3.0 | + 2.2 | + 2.0 |
| Men | 201,858 | 203,053 | 203,812 | 204,554 | + 0.6 | + 0.4 | + 0.4 |
| Women | 132,944 | 141,905 | 148,592 | 154,780 | + 6.7 | + 4.7 | + 4.2 |
| Two-year | 127,904 | 131,429 | 135,256 | 130,252 | + 2.8 | + 2.9 | − 3.7 |
| Men | 53,765 | 54,277 | 55,051 | 53,161 | + 1.0 | + 1.4 | − 3.4 |
| Women | 74,139 | 77,152 | 80,205 | 77,091 | + 4.1 | + 4.0 | − 3.9 |
| New | 394 | 8,088 | 15,120 | 22,240 | + 1,952.8 | + 86.9 | + 47.1 |
| Men | 294 | 5,745 | 9,755 | 13,569 | + 1,854.1 | + 69.8 | + 39.1 |
| Women | 100 | 2,343 | 5,365 | 8,671 | + 2,243.0 | + 129.0 | + 61.6 |

| | | | | | | | |
|---|---|---|---|---|---|---|---|
| **Private, Proprietary** | 71,304 | 111,714 | 152,235 | 176,954 | +56.7 | +36.3 | +16.2 |
| Men | 32,210 | 56,135 | 82,830 | 106,469 | +74.3 | +47.6 | +28.5 |
| Women | 39,094 | 55,579 | 69,405 | 70,485 | +42.2 | +24.9 | +1.6 |
| Doctoral | 0 | 0 | 0 | 0 | +0.0 | +0.0 | +0.0 |
| Men | 0 | 0 | 0 | 0 | +0.0 | +0.0 | +0.0 |
| Women | 0 | 0 | 0 | 0 | +0.0 | +0.0 | +0.0 |
| Comprehensive | 0 | 0 | 0 | 0 | +0.0 | +0.0 | +0.0 |
| Men | 0 | 0 | 0 | 0 | +0.0 | +0.0 | +0.0 |
| Women | 0 | 0 | 0 | 0 | +0.0 | +0.0 | +0.0 |
| General baccalaureate | 5,058 | 5,123 | 5,155 | 4,823 | +1.3 | +0.6 | -6.4 |
| Men | 2,336 | 2,295 | 2,319 | 2,149 | -1.8 | +1.0 | -7.3 |
| Women | 2,722 | 2,828 | 2,836 | 2,674 | +3.9 | +0.3 | -5.7 |
| Specialized | 13,545 | 18,290 | 21,106 | 22,666 | +35.0 | +15.4 | +7.4 |
| Men | 10,550 | 13,302 | 15,541 | 17,299 | +26.1 | +16.8 | +11.3 |
| Women | 2,995 | 4,988 | 5,565 | 5,367 | +66.5 | +11.6 | -3.6 |
| Two-year | 52,701 | 56,978 | 62,695 | 71,742 | +8.1 | +10.0 | +14.4 |
| Men | 19,324 | 19,254 | 22,011 | 26,855 | -0.4 | +14.3 | +22.0 |
| Women | 33,377 | 37,724 | 40,684 | 44,887 | 13.0 | +7.8 | +10.3 |
| New | 0 | 31,323 | 63,279 | 77,723 | +0.0 | +102.0 | +22.8 |
| Men | 0 | 21,284 | 42,959 | 60,166 | +0.0 | +101.8 | +40.1 |
| Women | 0 | 10,039 | 20,320 | 17,557 | +0.0 | +102.4 | -13.6 |

*Source:* U.S. Department of Education 1984d.

## A-4
## AID PER RECIPIENT AND NUMBERS OF RECIPIENTS
### (RECIPIENTS IN THOUSANDS)

| | 1980–81 | 1981–82 | Estimated 1982–83 | Estimated 1983–84 | Estimated 1984–85 | Percent Change 1980–81 to 1984–85 |
|---|---|---|---|---|---|---|
| **Pell Grant Program** | | | | | | |
| Recipients | 2,806 | 2,744 | 2,573 | 2,781 | 2,584 | –7.9 |
| Aid per recipient—current dollars | $851 | $838 | $941 | $1,001 | $1,073 | 26.1 |
| Aid per recipient—constant dollars | $948 | $859 | $925 | $950 | $971 | 2.4 |
| **SEOG Program** | | | | | | |
| Recipients | 717 | 659 | 636 | 648 | 686 | –4.3 |
| Aid per recipient—current dollars | $513 | $549 | $540 | $545 | $545 | 6.2 |
| Aid per recipient—constant dollars | $572 | $563 | $531 | $517 | $493 | –13.8 |
| **CWS Program** | | | | | | |
| Recipients | 819 | 739 | 721 | 800 | 759 | –7.3 |
| Aid per recipient—current dollars | $806 | $844 | $874 | $875 | $875 | 8.6 |
| Aid per recipient—constant dollars | $898 | $866 | $859 | $830 | $792 | –11.8 |
| **NDSL Program** | | | | | | |
| Recipients | 813 | 684 | 674 | 672 | 661 | –18.7 |
| Aid per recipient—current dollars | $853 | $848 | $882 | $885 | $885 | 3.8 |
| Aid per recipient—constant dollars | $951 | $870 | $867 | $840 | $801 | –15.8 |
| **GSL and PLUS Programs** | | | | | | |
| Recipients | 2,916 | 3,171 | 3,015 | 3,126 | 3,672 | 25.9 |
| Aid per recipient—current dollars | $2,128 | $2,304 | $2,192 | $2,495 | $2,306 | 8.4 |
| Aid per recipient—constant dollars | $2,371 | $2,363 | $2,155 | $2,368 | $2,087 | –12.0 |
| **State Grant and SSIG Programs** | | | | | | |
| Recipients | 1,140 | 1,448 | 1,493 | 1,524 | 1,565 | 37.3 |
| Aid per recipient—current dollars | $736 | $690 | $723 | $778 | $852 | 15.8 |
| Aid per recipient—constant dollars | $820 | $708 | $711 | $738 | $771 | –6.0 |

*Source:* College Board 1985, p. 6.

# RESOURCES AND EXPENDITURES FOR DEPENDENT AND INDEPENDENT AID-1 AND AID-2 RECIPIENTS, BY SEX[a]

| | Male | | | | Female | | | |
|---|---|---|---|---|---|---|---|---|
| | Dependent | | Independent | | Dependent | | Independent | |
| | AID-1 | AID-2 | AID-1 | AID-2 | AID-1 | AID-2 | AID-1 | AID-2 |
| **Resources** | | | | | | | | |
| Grants | | | | | | | | |
| 1981 | $1,260 | $ 75 | $1,357 | $ 95 | $1,220 | $ 151 | $1,320 | $ 318 |
| 1983 | 1,323 | 106 | 1,234 | 295 | 1,314 | 83 | 1,221 | 337 |
| Loans | | | | | | | | |
| 1981 | 873 | 2,359 | 1,035 | 2,968 | 718 | 2,359 | 669 | 2,590 |
| 1983 | 866 | 2,061 | 1,091 | 2,320 | 750 | 2,053 | 879 | 2,109 |
| Work | | | | | | | | |
| 1981 | 309 | 107 | 511 | 93 | 374 | 137 | 408 | 110 |
| 1983 | 374 | 54 | 536 | 195 | 393 | 21 | 486 | 118 |
| Other | | | | | | | | |
| 1981 | 126 | 29 | 123 | 67 | 85 | 47 | 107 | 118 |
| 1983 | 44 | 20 | 80 | 83 | 45 | 38 | 50 | 44 |
| Total | | | | | | | | |
| 1981 | 2,568 | 2,570 | 3,026 | 3,223 | 2,397 | 2,694 | 2,504 | 3,136 |
| 1983 | 2,607 | 2,241 | 2,941 | 2,893 | 2,500 | 2,205 | 2,635 | 2,589 |
| **Expenditures** | | | | | | | | |
| Tuition | | | | | | | | |
| 1981 | 1,056 | 1,129 | 826 | 1,052 | 936 | 1,089 | 724 | 861 |
| 1983 | 1,163 | 1,343 | 975 | 1,165 | 1,105 | 1,417 | 874 | 1,141 |
| Total | | | | | | | | |
| 1981 | 4,076 | 4,310 | 5,848 | 5,880 | 3,878 | 4,226 | 6,209 | 6,064 |
| 1983 | 4,282 | 4,683 | 5,961 | 5,963 | 4,174 | 4,713 | 6,208 | 6,178 |

[a]AID-1 recipients include students who receive aid from at least one federal, state, or institutional program according to the most stringent standards of needs analysis (that is, the standards for Pell Grants or uniform methodology). Roughly three out of four public college students whose aid is recorded in the files of campus student aid offices fall into this category.

AID-2 students also receive aid on the basis of need, but the standards for them are less stringent than for AID-1 recipients. Such students may also receive other forms of aid, but none from programs in the AID-1 category.

*Source:* Stampen 1985.

A-6

## DISTRIBUTION OF STUDENT AID BY GENDER AT INDEPENDENT INSTITUTIONS: 1981–82[a]

| Adjusted Gross Income | Tuition | Total Student Expenses | Expected Parental Contributions | Total Need-Based Grants[b] | Total Student Employment | Total Student Loans | Total Student Resources[c] | Balance[d] |
|---|---|---|---|---|---|---|---|---|
| **Under $6,000** | | | | | | | | |
| Male (N = 58,697) | | | | | | | | |
| Average dollar amount | $4,089 | $7,169 | $ 217 | $2,637 | $665 | $1,195 | $6,723 | –$ 446.00 |
| Percent of total expenses | 57.0 | 100.0 | 3.0 | 36.8 | 9.3 | 16.7 | 93.8 | –6.2 |
| Female (N = 47,427) | | | | | | | | |
| Average dollar amount | $3,682 | $6,447 | $ 102 | $2,821 | $386 | $ 927 | $5,648 | –$ 799.00 |
| Percent of total expenses | 56.3 | 100.0 | 1.6 | 43.8 | 6.0 | 14.4 | 87.6 | –12.4 |
| **$18,000 to $24,000** | | | | | | | | |
| Male (N = 58, 697) | | | | | | | | |
| Average dollar amount | $4,134 | $7,173 | $ 886 | $2,348 | $564 | $1,449 | $6,815 | –$ 358.00 |
| Percent of total expenses | 57.6 | 100.0 | 12.4 | 32.7 | 7.9 | 20.2 | 95.0 | –5.0 |
| Female (N = 62,241) | | | | | | | | |
| Average dollar amount | $4,100 | $7,031 | $ 908 | $2,186 | $595 | $1,283 | $6,277 | –$ 754.00 |
| Percent of total expenses | 58.3 | 100.0 | 12.9 | 31.1 | 8.5 | 18.3 | 89.3 | –10.7 |
| **$36,000 or More** | | | | | | | | |
| Male (N = 59,819) | | | | | | | | |
| Average dollar amount | $4,726 | $8,042 | $4,371 | $1,146 | $468 | $1,927 | $9,625 | $1,582.00 |
| Percent of total expenses | 58.8 | 100.0 | 54.4 | 14.2 | 5.8 | 24.0 | 199.7 | 19.7 |
| Female (N = 65,107) | | | | | | | | |
| Average dollar amount | $4,653 | $7,956 | $4,307 | $1,144 | $418 | $1,808 | $9,085 | $1,129.00 |
| Percent of total expenses | 58.5 | 100.0 | 54.1 | 14.4 | 5.3 | 22.7 | 114.2 | 14.2 |

[a]Sample is based on undergraduate dependent students only.
[b]Need-based grants include Pell Grants, Supplemental Educational Opportunity Grants, state grants, and institutional grants.
[c]Total student resources include expected student contributions and other aid in addition to expected parental contributions, total grants, total employment, and total loans.
[d]Total resources minus total expenses.

*Source:* National Institute of Independent Colleges and Universities 1983.

## CIRP FIRST-TIME, FULL-TIME STUDENT FINANCING SOURCES, BY SEX AND MAJOR CATEGORIES: 1973–74 THROUGH 1979–80

| | | 1973–74 | | 1974–75 | | 1975–76 | | 1976–77 | | 1977–78 | | 1978–79 | | 1979–80 | |
|---|---|---|---|---|---|---|---|---|---|---|---|---|---|---|---|
| **Number in Sample**[a] | M | 18,310 | | 17,987 | | 16,608 | | 19,367 | | 17,427 | | 16,637 | | 17,333 | |
| | F | 17,095 | | 17,365 | | 16,493 | | 19,359 | | 18,514 | | 17,667 | | 17,850 | |
| **Finance Category** | | $ | % | $ | % | $ | % | $ | % | $ | % | $ | % | $ | % |
| Own savings/earnings | M | 646.42 | 33.2 | 634.58 | 31.7 | 597.03 | 28.8 | 638.30 | 28.5 | 647.84 | 27.3 | 702.07 | 22.6 | 629.32 | 20.6 |
| | F | 432.39 | 23.4 | 467.33 | 24.2 | 440.82 | 21.7 | 470.82 | 22.0 | 482.43 | 21.5 | 545.46 | 17.8 | 503.36 | 17.1 |
| Support of family/friends | M | 721.87 | 37.1 | 799.64 | 39.9 | 822.51 | 39.7 | 889.55 | 39.7 | 931.95 | 39.2 | 1,448.24 | 46.7 | 1,381.16 | 45.3 |
| | F | 903.74 | 49.0 | 943.79 | 48.8 | 984.02 | 48.4 | 974.68 | 45.6 | 1,015.46 | 45.2 | 1,598.44 | 52.3 | 1,469.02 | 49.8 |
| Scholarships/grants | M | 321.83 | 16.5 | 381.41 | 19.0 | 427.55 | 20.6 | 472.46 | 21.1 | 512.98 | 21.6 | 578.48 | 18.7 | 601.36 | 19.7 |
| | F | 269.86 | 14.6 | 350.08 | 18.1 | 420.50 | 20.7 | 463.09 | 21.7 | 509.84 | 22.7 | 568.22 | 18.6 | 603.58 | 20.5 |
| Loans | M | 195.41 | 10.0 | 142.50 | 7.1 | 166.35 | 8.0 | 204.24 | 9.1 | 237.59 | 10.0 | 302.78 | 9.8 | 367.09 | 12.0 |
| | F | 214.29 | 11.6 | 150.70 | 7.8 | 168.38 | 8.3 | 201.97 | 9.5 | 210.04 | 9.3 | 307.55 | 10.1 | 341.64 | 11.6 |
| Other | M | 61.37 | 3.2 | 44.83 | 2.2 | 59.66 | 2.9 | 36.48 | 1.6 | 45.18 | 1.9 | 68.54 | 2.2 | 69.38 | 2.3 |
| | F | 25.52 | 1.4 | 20.10 | 1.0 | 19.20 | 0.9 | 24.69 | 1.2 | 28.98 | 1.3 | 37.87 | 1.2 | 33.58 | 1.1 |
| **Total** | M | 1,946.90 | 100.0 | 2,002.96 | 100.0 | 2,073.10 | 100.0 | 2,241.03 | 100.0 | 2,375.54 | 100.0 | 3,100.11 | 100.0 | 3,048.31 | 100.0 |
| | F | 1,845.80 | 100.0 | 1,932.00 | 100.0 | 2,032.92 | 100.0 | 2,135.25 | 100.0 | 2,246.75 | 100.0 | 3,057.54 | 100.0 | 2,951.18 | 100.0 |

[a]Represents a 20 percent sample of the national first-time, full-time higher education enrollment. Data are weighted values.

*Source:* Leslie 1982.

## A-8

## EXPENSES AND SOURCES OF SUPPORT FOR INDEPENDENT RECIPIENTS OF NEED-BASED AID: 1981–82

| | Independent Institutions | | Public Institutions | | Proprietary Institutions | |
|---|---|---|---|---|---|---|
| | Average Dollars[a] | Percent of Total Costs | Average Dollars[a] | Percent of Total Costs | Average Dollars[a] | Percent of Total costs |
| **Student Expenses** | | | | | | |
| Tuition, fees | $3,326 | | $ 702 | | $2,831 | |
| Other | 4,898 | | 5,423 | | 4,578 | |
| Total, expenses | $8,224 | 100% | $6,125 | 100% | $7,410 | 100% |
| **Student Resources** | | | | | | |
| Parental contribution | $ 136 | 2% | $ 11 | 0% | $ 0 | 0% |
| Grants (need-based) | | | | | | |
| Pell | $1,169 | 14% | $ 832 | 14% | $1,101 | 15% |
| SEOG | 76 | 1 | 146 | 2 | 126 | 1 |
| State (including SSIG) | 1,013 | 12 | 158 | 2 | 54 | 1 |
| Institutional | 374 | 5 | 31 | 1 | 0 | 0 |
| Total, grants | $2,632 | 32% | $1,168 | 19% | $1,281 | 17% |
| Student employment | | | | | | |
| College Work Study | $ 231 | 3% | 276 | 4% | $ 35 | 1% |
| State/institutional | 95 | 1 | 171 | 3 | 74 | 1 |
| Total, employment | $ 326 | 4% | $ 447 | 7% | $ 109 | 2% |
| Loans | | | | | | |
| NDSL | $ 143 | 2% | $ 161 | 3% | $ 263 | 4% |
| GSL/FISL | 734 | 9 | 534 | 9 | 1,221 | 16 |
| Institutional | 44 | 0 | 17 | 0 | 13 | 0 |
| Total, loans | $ 921 | 11% | $ 712 | 12% | $1,497 | 20% |
| Student contribution | $2,096 | 26% | $1,959 | 32% | $2,070 | 28% |
| Other aid | $ 667 | 8% | $ 339 | 6% | $ 292 | 4% |
| Total, all resources | $6,777 | 82% | $4,636 | 76% | $5,249 | 71% |
| **Balance: Remaining Need** | $1,447 | 18% | $1,488 | 24% | $2,160 | 29% |

[a]Each dollar figure is an average; individual averages do not add precisely to subtotal and total averages.

Source: El-Khawas 1983.

## EXPENSES AND SOURCES OF SUPPORT FOR DEPENDENT RECIPIENTS OF NEED-BASED AID: 1981–82

| | Independent Institutions | | Public Institutions | | Proprietary Institutions | |
|---|---|---|---|---|---|---|
| | Average Dollars[a] | Percent of Total Costs | Average Dollars[a] | Percent of Total Costs | Average Dollars[a] | Percent of Total Costs |
| **Student Expenses** | | | | | | |
| Tuition, fees | $4,190 | | $ 921 | | $2,815 | |
| Other | 3,039 | | 2,912 | | 2,733 | |
| Total, expenses | $7,229 | 100% | $3,833 | 100% | $5,548 | 100% |
| **Student Resources** | | | | | | |
| Parental contribution | $1,305 | 18% | $ 469 | 12% | $ 481 | 9% |
| Grants (need-based) | | | | | | |
| Pell | $ 529 | 7% | $ 714 | 19% | $ 970 | 18% |
| SEOG | 222 | 3 | 117 | 3 | 128 | 2 |
| State (including SSIG) | 611 | 9 | 159 | 4 | 128 | 2 |
| Institutional | 822 | 11 | 43 | 1 | 2 | 0 |
| Total, grants | $2,185 | 30% | $1,033 | 27% | $1,228 | 22% |
| Student employment | | | | | | |
| College Work Study | $ 428 | 6% | $ 252 | 7% | $ 66 | 1% |
| State/institutional | 124 | 2 | 94 | 2 | 39 | 1 |
| Total, employment | $ 551 | 8% | $ 346 | 9% | $ 104 | 2% |
| Loans | | | | | | |
| NDSL | $ 339 | 5% | $ 156 | 4% | $ 225 | 4% |
| GSL/FISL | 1,110 | 15 | 555 | 15 | 1,235 | 22 |
| Institutional | 21 | 0 | 8 | 0 | 8 | 0 |
| Total, loans | $1,470 | 20% | $ 719 | 19% | $1,468 | 26% |
| Student contribution | $ 891 | 12% | $ 540 | 14% | $ 423 | 8% |
| Other aid | $ 569 | 8% | $ 282 | 7% | $ 193 | 4% |
| Total, all resources | $6,972 | 97% | $3,390 | 88% | $3,897 | 70% |
| **Balance: Remaining Need** | $ 257 | 3% | $ 443 | 12% | $1,651 | 30% |

[a]Each dollar figure is an average; individual averages do not add precisely to subtotal and total averages.

*Source:* El-Khawas 1983.

## A-10
## LABOR FORCE STATUS OF WOMEN, AGE 25 TO 64, BY YEARS OF SCHOOL COMPLETED: MARCH 1984
### (NUMBERS IN THOUSANDS)

| | Total | Percent of Total | Women | Percent of Women |
|---|---|---|---|---|
| **Civilian Noninstitutional Population** | 113,893 | 100.0 | 58,901 | 100.0 |
| Elementary | | | | |
| 8 years or less | 10,618 | 9.3 | 5,059 | 8.6 |
| High school | | | | |
| 1 to 3 years | 13,197 | 11.6 | 7,064 | 12.0 |
| 4 years only | 46,209 | 40.6 | 26,310 | 44.7 |
| College | | | | |
| 1 to 3 years | 19,636 | 17.2 | 10,100 | 17.1 |
| 4 years or more | 24,232 | 21.3 | 10,368 | 17.6 |
| **Civilian Labor Force** | 86,001 | 100.0 | 37,234 | 100.0 |
| Elementary | | | | |
| 8 years or less | 5,818 | 6.8 | 1,917 | 5.1 |
| High school | | | | |
| 1 to 3 years | 8,545 | 9.9 | 3,472 | 9.3 |
| 4 years only | 34,603 | 40.2 | 16,709 | 44.9 |
| College | | | | |
| 1 to 3 years | 15,812 | 18.4 | 7,050 | 18.9 |
| 4 years or more | 21,223 | 24.7 | 8,086 | 21.7 |
| **Labor Force Participation Rate** | 75.5 | | 63.2 | |
| Elementary | | | | |
| 8 years or less | 54.8 | | 37.9 | |
| High school | | | | |
| 1 to 3 years | 64.7 | | 49.1 | |
| 4 years only | 74.9 | | 63.5 | |
| College | | | | |
| 1 to 3 years | 80.5 | | 69.8 | |
| 4 years or more | 87.6 | | 78.0 | |

## A-10 (continued)

| | Total | Percent of Total | Women | Percent of Women |
|---|---|---|---|---|
| **Employed** | 80,365 | 100.0 | 34,953 | 100.0 |
| Elementary | | | | |
| 8 years or less | 5,144 | 6.4 | 1,691 | 4.8 |
| High school | | | | |
| 1 to 3 years | 7,488 | 9.3 | 3,070 | 8.8 |
| 4 years only | 32,097 | 39.9 | 15,646 | 44.8 |
| College | | | | |
| 1 to 3 years | 14,980 | 18.6 | 6,678 | 19.1 |
| 4 years or more | 20,655 | 25.7 | 7,868 | 22.5 |
| **Unemployed** | 5,635 | 100.0 | 2,280 | 100.0 |
| Elementary | | | | |
| 8 years or less | 675 | 12.0 | 226 | 9.9 |
| High school | | | | |
| 1 to 3 years | 1,056 | 18.7 | 401 | 17.6 |
| 4 years only | 2,505 | 44.5 | 1,061 | 46.5 |
| College | | | | |
| 1 to 3 years | 831 | 14.7 | 372 | 16.3 |
| 4 years or more | 568 | 10.1 | 218 | 9.6 |
| **Unemployment Rate** | 6.6 | | 6.1 | |
| Elementary | | | | |
| 8 years or less | 11.6 | | 11.8 | |
| High school | | | | |
| 1 to 3 years | 12.4 | | 11.5 | |
| 4 years only | 7.2 | | 6.3 | |
| College | | | | |
| 1 to 3 years | 5.3 | | 5.3 | |
| 4 years or more | 2.7 | | 2.7 | |

*Source:* U.S. Department of Labor 1985.

## PERSONS 22 YEARS OLD AND OVER BELOW POVERTY LEVEL, BY AGE GROUP, EDUCATIONAL ATTAINMENT, SEX, AND RACE: 1981

| Years of School Completed | Number below Poverty Level[a] (000) | | | | Poverty Rate | | | |
|---|---|---|---|---|---|---|---|---|
| | Total | 22–34 Years Old | 35–64 Years Old | 65 Years Old and Over | Total | 22–34 Years Old | 35–64 Years Old | 65 Years Old and Over |
| **Total** | 16,732 | 6,074 | 6,805 | 3,853 | 11.3 | 11.8 | 9.5 | 15.3 |
| 5 years or less | 2,013 | 196 | 865 | 952 | 35.2 | 35.3 | 34.5 | 35.9 |
| 6 to 8 years | 3,480 | 548 | 1,451 | 1,482 | 21.6 | 33.9 | 20.2 | 20.3 |
| 9 to 11 years | 3,622 | 1,413 | 1,577 | 632 | 18.6 | 27.8 | 15.4 | 15.2 |
| 12 years | 5,049 | 2,465 | 2,043 | 542 | 8.8 | 11.4 | 7.0 | 8.3 |
| 1 or more years of college | 2,568 | 1,453 | 871 | 245 | 5.2 | 6.5 | 3.8 | 5.4 |
| **Male** | 6,001 | 2,361 | 2,559 | 1,080 | 8.6 | 9.3 | 7.4 | 10.5 |
| 5 years or less | 839 | 83 | 392 | 364 | 29.1 | 29.1 | 29.3 | 28.9 |
| 6 to 8 years | 1,144 | 213 | 561 | 370 | 15.5 | 27.4 | 15.4 | 12.4 |
| 9 to 11 years | 1,140 | 471 | 500 | 169 | 13.1 | 19.6 | 10.7 | 10.4 |
| 12 years | 1,736 | 915 | 709 | 112 | 7.1 | 9.0 | 5.9 | 4.8 |
| 1 or more years of college | 1,140 | 679 | 398 | 65 | 4.3 | 5.8 | 3.1 | 3.1 |
| **Female** | 10,731 | 3,713 | 4,246 | 2,773 | 13.7 | 14.2 | 11.4 | 18.6 |
| 5 years or less | 1,174 | 112 | 473 | 588 | 41.4 | 41.5 | 40.3 | 42.3 |
| 6 to 8 years | 2,336 | 336 | 889 | 1,112 | 26.9 | 40.1 | 25.1 | 25.8 |
| 9 to 11 years | 2,482 | 942 | 1,076 | 463 | 23.0 | 35.2 | 19.4 | 18.2 |
| 12 years | 3,313 | 1,550 | 1,334 | 429 | 10.1 | 13.5 | 7.9 | 10.2 |
| 1 or more years of college | 1,427 | 774 | 473 | 180 | 6.1 | 7.2 | 4.7 | 7.3 |

# A-11 (continued)

| | Number below Poverty Level[a] (000) | | | | Poverty Rate | | | |
|---|---|---|---|---|---|---|---|---|
| **White** | 12,066 | 4,243 | 4,845 | 2,978 | 9.3 | 9.7 | 7.7 | 13.1 |
| 5 years or less | 1,267 | 160 | 550 | 558 | 30.9 | 32.9 | 30.8 | 30.4 |
| 6 to 8 years | 2,604 | 407 | 995 | 1,202 | 19.0 | 30.8 | 17.0 | 18.5 |
| 9 to 11 years | 2,392 | 876 | 1,004 | 512 | 14.8 | 21.8 | 12.1 | 13.4 |
| 12 years | 3,786 | 1,711 | 1,583 | 492 | 7.4 | 9.2 | 6.0 | 7.9 |
| 1 or more years of college | 2,016 | 1,088 | 714 | 214 | 4.5 | 5.6 | 3.5 | 4.9 |
| **Black** | 4,154 | 1,591 | 1,743 | 820 | 27.3 | 26.3 | 24.7 | 39.0 |
| 5 years or less | 655 | 16 | 271 | 368 | 49.3 | b | 46.6 | 51.9 |
| 6 to 8 years | 797 | 116 | 410 | 271 | 38.3 | 47.5 | 35.4 | 39.6 |
| 9 to 11 years | 1,142 | 498 | 539 | 105 | 37.6 | 51.7 | 30.7 | 32.5 |
| 12 years | 1,116 | 655 | 413 | 48 | 21.6 | 24.5 | 18.3 | 21.0 |
| 1 or more years of college | 441 | 306 | 108 | 27 | 12.3 | 14.3 | 8.3 | 17.3 |

[a]Income for 1981 as reported in March 1982.
[b]Base less than 75,000.

Source: U.S. Department of Education 1984c.

## A-12

## PERCENTAGE OF SCHOLASTIC APTITUDE TEST SCORES OVER 600 IN MATHEMATICS, BY GENDER: 1973–1981

| | 1973 | | 1974 | | 1975 | | 1976 | | 1977 | | 1978 | | 1979 | | 1980 | | 1981 | |
|---|---|---|---|---|---|---|---|---|---|---|---|---|---|---|---|---|---|---|
| | M | F | M | F | M | F | M | F | M | F | M | F | M | F | M | F | M | F |
| 700–800 | 4 | 1 | 6 | 1 | 6 | 1 | 6 | 1 | 6 | 1 | 6 | 1 | 5 | 1 | 4 | 1 | 4 | 1 |
| 600–699 | 17 | 9 | 17 | 10 | 16 | 9 | 17 | 9 | 16 | 9 | 16 | 9 | 16 | 8 | 16 | 9 | 16 | 8 |

*Source:* Gordon and Addison 1985, p. 72.

# APPENDIX B

## FINANCIAL ASSISTANCE SOURCES FOR WOMEN

The following list of publications and organizations is designed to aid women seeking financial assistance for higher education. All prices are subject to change; please check with the organization listed for current price. More information can be obtained by writing to the publishers and organizations listed below. (This list was adapted from *Financial Aid: A Partial List of Resources for Women*, listed below.)

### Publications

*Better Late Than Never: Financial Aid for Older Women Seeking Education and Training*, Women's Equity Action League. 805 15th Street NW, Suite 822, Washington DC 20005: 1986. $8.00

*Directory of Financial Aid for Women*, 3d edition, Gail Ann Schlachter. ABC-Clio, 2040 A.P.S. Box 4397, Santa Barbara CA 93103: 1984. $35.00

*The Directory of Special Opportunities for Women*, Matha Merrill Doxx, ed. Garrett Park Press, Garrett Park MD 20896: 1981. $19.00

*Educational Financial Aids*, American Association of University Women. 2401 Virginia Avenue NW, Washington DC 20037: 1981. $5.00

*Financial Aid: A Partial List of Resources for Women*, Project on the Status and Education of WOMEN, Association of American Colleges. 1818 R Street NW, Washington DC 20009: 1984. $2.50

*Higher Education Opportunities for Minorities and Women*, U.S. Department of Education. U.S. Government Printing Office, Washington DC 20402: 1985. $2.50

*How to Get Money for Research*, Mary Rubin. The Feminist Press, P.O. Box 1654, Hagerstown, MD 21741: 1983. $5.95

*Professional Women's Groups*, American Association of University Women. 2401 Virginia Avenue NW, Washington DC 20037. $3.00

*Resources for Women in Science*, Association for Women in Science. 1346 Connecticut Avenue NW, Room 1122, Washington DC 20036: 1980. Free (SASE)

### Organizations

American Association of University Women Educational Foundation, 2401 Virginia Avenue NW, Washington DC 20037.

Business and Professional Women's Foundation, 2012 Massachusetts Avenue NW, Washington DC 20036.

Center for Continuing Education for Women, University of Michigan, Ann Arbor MI 48109.

General Federation of Women's Clubs, 1734 N Street NW, Washington DC 20036.

Jewish Foundation for the Education of Women, 330 W. 58th Street, New York NY 10019.

National Federation of Press Women, Professional Education Scholarships, Box 99, Blue Springs MO 64015.

National Society of the Daughters of the American Revolution, Office of the Committees, 1776 D Street NW, Washington DC 20006.

Office of Women in Higher Education, American Council on Education, One Dupont Circle, Suite 800, Washington DC 20036.

Society of Women Engineers, United Engineering Center, Room 305, 345 E. 47th Street, New York NY 10017.

U.S. Department of Health and Human Services, Student and Institutional Assistance Branch, Division of Student Assistance, Parklawn Building, Room 8-44, Rockville MD 20857.

# REFERENCES

The ERIC Clearinghouse on Higher Education abstracts and indexes the current literature on higher education for the Office of Educational Research and Improvement's monthly bibliographic journal, *Resources in Education*. Most of these publications are available through the ERIC Document Reproduction Service (EDRS). For publications cited in this bibliography that are available from EDRS, ordering number and price are included. Readers who wish to order a publication should write to the ERIC Document Reproduction Service, 3900 Wheeler Avenue, Alexandria, Virginia 22304. When ordering, please specify the document number. Documents are available as noted in microfiche (MF) and paper copy (PC). Because prices are subject to change, it is advisable to check the latest issue of *Resources in Education* for current cost based on the number of pages in the publication.

Abramovitz, Mimi. 1977. *Where Are the Women? A Study of Worker Underutilization of Tuition Refund Plans*. Ithaca, N.Y.: Cornell University, Institute for Education and Research on Women and Work.

Academic Financial Services Association. 1985. *A New Generation in Student Information Systems*. Long Beach, Cal.: Author.

American Association of State Colleges and Universities. 1974. *Women's Stake in Low Tuition*. Washington, D.C.: Author. ED 096 933. 20 pp. MF–$1.00; PC–$3.59.

American Association of University Women, 1985. "Women and Student Financial Aid." Policy Brief. Washington, D.C.: Author.

American Bar Association. 1984. *A Review of Legal Education in the United States, Fall 1983: Law Schools and Bar Admission Requirements*. Chicago: American Bar Association, Section of Legal Education and Admissions to the Bar.

American College Testing Student Needs Analysis Service. 1974 to 1980. *National Norms for ACT Financial Aid Applicants*. Computer printouts for various years. Iowa City: American College Testing.

American Legion. 1985. *Need a Lift? To Educational Opportunities, Careers, Loans, Scholarships, Employment*. Indianapolis: Author.

Andersen, Charles J. 1986. *Student Financial Aid to Full-time Undergraduates, Fall 1984*. Higher Education Panel Report No. 68. Washington, D.C.: American Council on Education. ED 266 718. 33 pp. MF–$1.00; PC$5.14.

Astin, Alexander. 1975. *Financial Aid and Student Persistence*. Los Angeles: University of California, Higher Education Research Institute.

———. 1982. *The American Freshman, 1966–1981: Some Implications for Educational Policy and Practice*. Prepared for the National Commission on Excellence in Education. Los Angeles: University of California, Higher Education Research Institute. ED 227 070. 59 pp. MF–$1.00; PC–$7.29.

Astin, Alexander W.; Green, Kenneth C.; Korn, William S.; and Schalit, Marilyn. 1985. *The American Freshman: National Norms for Fall 1985*. Los Angeles: University of California, Higher Education Research Institute. ED 265 778. 249 pp. MF–$1.00; PC not available EDRS.

Atwell, Robert H.; Grimes, Bruce; and Lopiano, Donna. 1980. *The Money Game: Financing Collegiate Athletics*. Washington, D.C.: American Council on Education.

Bailey, Susan. 1983. "A Concern about Sex Equitable Education for Disabled Students." *Concerns*. Washington, D.C.: Council of Chief State School Officers.

Berkshire, Linda. 1983. Testimony on behalf of the National Student Aid Coalition before the Subcommittee on Postsecondary Education, Committee on Education and Labor, U.S. House of Representatives, 27 October, Washington, D.C.

———. 1985. *A Description of the Uniform Methodology: Needs Analysis for Determining Student Aid Eligibility*. Washington, D.C.: National Student Aid Coalition.

Binder, Shirley S. 1983. "Meeting Student Needs with Different Types of Financial Aid Awards." In *Handbook of Student Financial Aid,* edited by Robert H. Fenske and Robert P. Huff. San Francisco: Jossey-Bass.

Bluestone, Barry, and Harrison, Bennett. 1982. *The Deindustrialization of America: Plant Closings, Community Abandonment, and the Dismantling of Basic Industry*. New York: Basic Books.

Bob, Sharon. May 1977. "The Myth of Equality: Financial Support for Males and Females." *Journal of College Student Personnel* 18: 235–38.

Bogart, Karen. 1981. *Institutional Self-Study Guide on Sex Equity for Postsecondary Educational Institutions*. Washington, D.C.: American Institutes for Research.

Bogart, Karen; Flagle, Judith; and Jung, Steve. 1974. *Institutional Self-Study Guide on Sex Equity for Postsecondary Educational Institutions*. Washington, D.C.: American Institutes for Research.

Boyan, Douglas R., ed. 1983. *Profiles: The Foreign Student in the United States*. New York: Institute of International Education. ED 262 704. 242 pp. MF–$1.00; PC not available EDRS.

Boyd, Joseph D., and Martin, Dennis J. 1986. *The NASFAA Loan Study: A Report on the Characteristics of GSL Borrowers*

*and the Impact of Educational Debt.* Washington, D.C.:
National Association of Student Financial Aid Administrators.

Breneman, David W., and Nelson, Susan C. 1981. *Financing Community Colleges: An Economic Perspective.* Washington, D.C.: Brookings Institution. ED 211 151. 222 pp. MF–$1.00; PC–$18.81.

Brooks, Adree. 16 October 1983. "For the Woman: Strides and Snags." National Employment Report. *The New York Times.*

Bruns, Ruth Ketchum. 1984. *The NASFAA Encyclopedia of Student Financial Aid.* Washington, D.C.: National Association of Student Financial Aid Administrators.

Butler-Nalin, Paul; Sanderson, Allen; and Redman, David. 1983. *Financing Graduate Education: Graduate Student Borrowing, Needs of the Disadvantaged and Underrepresented, and the Climate for Graduate Study.* Washington, D.C.: Consortium on Financing Higher Education. Prepared for the National Commission on Student Financial Assistance.

Caliendo, Nat, and Curtice, John K. May 1977. "Title IX: A Guide for Financial Aid Administrators." *Journal of Student Financial Aid* 7: 35.

California Student Aid Commission. 1984. *A Report on the Bilingual Teacher Grant Program for the Academic Year 1983–84.* Sacramento: Author.

Campbell, Nancy; Greenberger, Marcia; Kohn, Margaret; and Wilchner, Shirley. 1983. *Sex Discrimination in Education: Legal Rights and Remedies.* Washington, D.C.: National Women's Law Center.

Carnegie Commission on Higher Education. 1968. *Quality and Equality: New Levels of Federal Responsibility for Higher Education.* New York: McGraw-Hill.

Carnegie Council on Policy Studies in Higher Education. 1977. *Higher Education: Who Pays? Who Benefits? Who Should Pay?* New York: McGraw-Hill.

———. 1979. *Next Steps for the 1980s in Student Financial Aid.* San Francisco: Jossey-Bass. ED 172 597. 77 pp. MF–$1.00; PC not available EDRS.

Carroll, C. Dennis. 1983. *Tabulation of Student Financial Aid Statistics for the High School Class of 1980 Who Attended Postsecondary Education in Academic Year 1980–81.* Washington, D.C.: U.S. Department of Education, National Center for Education Statistics.

Case, Joe Paul. 1983. "Determining Financial Need." In *Handbook of Student Financial Aid,* edited by Robert H. Fenske and Robert P. Huff. San Francisco: Jossey-Bass.

*Chronicle of Higher Education.* 5 September 1984. "NCAA

Admits Difficulty in Catching Violators of Recruiting and Financial Aid Regulations'' 29: 33.

Clohan, William C. 1985. *Guaranteed Student Loan Program: Overview, History, Policy Issues, and Recommendations for Reauthorization.* Arlington, Va.: Consumer Bankers Association.

College Board. 1985. *Trends in Student Aid: 1980 to 1984.* Washington, D.C.: Author. HE 019 569. 14 pp. MF–$1.00; PC–$3.59.

College Entrance Examination Board. 1980 to 1986. *SAT Annual Reports.* New York: Author.

*Congressional Record.* 12 September 1984. ''Proceedings and Debates of the 98th Congress, Second Session'' 130 (113): S11034.

————. 3 October 1984. ''Proceedings and Debates of the 98th Congress, Second Session'' 130 (129): S12906.

Congressional Research Service. 1985. *Reauthorization of the Higher Education Act: Program Descriptions, Issues, and Options.* Washington, D.C.: Library of Congress.

Cooperative Institutional Research Program. 1982. Tabulations from freshman norm data. The Higher Education Research Institute, Los Angeles: University of California.

Cowans, David. 1975. Testimony during hearings on the Bankruptcy Act Revision before the Committee on the Judiciary, Subcommittee on Civil and Constitutional Rights, U.S. House of Representatives, 12 September, Washington, D.C.

Cross, K. Patricia. 1976. ''The Woman Student.'' In *Women in Higher Education,* edited by Todd Furniss and Patricia Graham. Washington, D.C.: American Council on Education.

Cross, K. Patricia, and McCartan, Anne-Marie. 1984. *Adult Learning: State Policies and Institutional Practices.* ASHE-ERIC Higher Education Report No. 1. Washington, D.C.: Association for the Study of Higher Education. ED 246 831. 162 pp. MF–$1.00; PC–$15.52.

Davis, Jerry. November 1977. ''Paying for College Costs: Does the Student's Sex Make a Difference?'' *Journal of Student Financial Aid* 7: 21–34.

————. 1983. *The Impact of State Student Incentive Grant Program Funds on the Implementation, Maintenance, and Growth of State-Supported Student Grant Programs.* Harrisburg: Pennsylvania Higher Education Assistance Agency.

————. 1983. *A Profession in Transition: Characteristics and Attitudes of the Financial Aid Administrator, Fall 1981.* Washington, D.C.: National Association of Student Financial Aid Administrators.

―――. 1985. *Ten Facts about Defaults in the Guaranteed Student Loan Program.* Harrisburg: Pennsylvania Higher Education Assistance Agency.

Deane, Robert T. 1980. *Study of Program Management Procedures in the Campus-Based and Basic Grant Programs.* Summary Final Report. Washington, D.C.: Applied Management Sciences.

Dexter, David. 1984. *Annual Debt Collection Report to Congress.* Washington, D.C.: U.S. Department of Education, Office of Credit Management Improvement.

Dunkle, Margaret C. 1980. *Financial Aid: Helping Re-entry Women Pay College Costs.* Washington, D.C.: Project on the Status and Education of Women. ED 193 980. 16 pp. MF–$1.00; PC–$3.59.

Edsall, Thomas B. 1984. *The New Politics of Inequality.* New York: W. W. Norton & Co.

Educational Testing Service. 1984. *National Report on College-Bound Seniors, 1984.* New York: College Entrance Examination Board.

El-Khawas, Elaine. 1983. *Comparison Data from Public, Independent, and Proprietary Institutions.* Tables compiled for policy seminar sponsored by the American Council on Education and the National Commission on Student Financial Assistance, 3 June, Washington, D.C.

*Federal Register.* 1978 to 1985. "Annual Indexes for Student Aid Regulations." Washington, D.C.: U.S. Government Printing Office.

Fenske, Robert; Hearn, James; and Curry, Denis. 1985. *Unmet Student Financial Need in the State of Washington: A Study of the "Need Gap."* Olympia: State of Washington Council for Postsecondary Education. ED 262 694. 67 pp. MF–$1.00; PC–$7.29.

Fife, Jonathan D. 1975. *Applying the Goals of Student Financial Aid.* AAHE-ERIC Higher Education Research Report No. 10. Washington, D.C.: American Association for Higher Education. ED 118 052. 76 pp. MF–$1.00; PC–$9.56.

Flamer, Herbert; Horch, Dwight; and Davis, Susan. 1982. *Talented and Needy Graduate and Professional Students: A National Survey of People Who Applied for Need-Based Financial Aid to Attend Graduate School or Professional School in 1980–81.* Princeton, N.J.: Educational Testing Service.

Fleming, Jacqueline; Payne, Kathleen; and Kirschner, Alan K. 1984. *United Negro College Fund Statistical Report of the Member Institutions.* New York: United Negro College Fund.

---

Frances, Carol. 1985. *The Escalating Cost of Higher Education: Impacts on States and Students*. Denver: Education Commission of the States.

Friedland, Sandra. 21 August 1983. "For Minority Engineers, A GEM of a Program." *The New York Times Summer Survey of Education*.

Furniss, W. Todd, and Graham, Patricia A. 1974. *Women in Higher Education*. Washington, D.C.: American Council on Education.

Gardner, David P. August/September 1982. "A Time for Reexamination and Renewal of Commitment." *American Education* 3: 34.

―――. 1983. Transcripts of public hearing of the Appropriate Balance Subcommittee, 14 January, at the University of Utah, Salt Lake City. Washington, D.C.: National Archives.

Gladen, James. 1983. Presentation at the Legal Training Conference on Educational Equity of the National Women's Law Center, 18 October, Washington, D.C.

Gladieux, Lawrence E., and Wolanin, Thomas R. 1976. *Congress and the Colleges*. Lexington, Mass.: Lexington Books.

Gordon, Barbara J. A., and Addison, Linda. 1985. "Gifted Girls and Women in Education." In *Handbook for Achieving Sex Equity through Education,* edited by Susan S. Klein. Baltimore: Johns Hopkins University Press.

*Grove City College* v. *Bell,* 687 F.2d 684 (3d Cir. 1982), *aff'd,* 104 S. Ct. 1211 (1984).

Gruss, Emily, and Hauptman, Arthur. 1985. *Closing the Information Gap: Ways to Improve Student Awareness of Financial Aid Opportunities*. Washington, D.C.: National Student Aid Coalition.

Guttmacher Institute. 1985. *Teenage Pregnancy: The Problem That Hasn't Gone Away*. Washington, D.C.: Author.

Hansen, Janet S. 1983. *Another Look at SSIG*. Prepared for the National Commission on Student Financial Assistance. Washington, D.C.: College Board. ED 228 946. 22 pp. MF–$1.00; PC–$3.59.

Hansen, Janet S., and Franklin, Paul L. 1984. *College Opportunity and Public Assistance Programs: Ideas for Resolving Conflicts*. Washington, D.C.: College Board.

Hauptman, Arthur. 1976. "Student Loan Defaults: Toward a Better Understanding of the Problem." In *Student Loans: Problems and Policy Alternatives,* edited by Lois Rice. New York: College Entrance Examination Board. ED 143 244. 180 pp. MF–$1.00; PC–$17.79.

Hechinger, Fred M. 28 January 1986. "Dark Side of Student Loans to Needy." *The New York Times*.

Henry, Fran Worden. 1983. *Toughing It Out at Harvard: The Making of a Woman MBA*. New York: G. P. Putnam's Sons.

Higher Education Research Institute. 1982. *Final Report of the Commission on the Higher Education of Minorities*. San Francisco: Jossey-Bass. ED 224 857. 47 pp. MF–$1.00; PC–$5.46.

Hill, Susan. 1983. *Participation of Black Students in Higher Education: A Statistical Profile from 1970–71 to 1980–81*. Washington, D.C.: U.S. Department of Education, National Center for Education Statistics.

Hornig, Lilli. 1983. Testimony before the National Commission on Student Financial Assistance, Subcommittee on Graduate Education, 15 March, at New York University. Washington, D.C.: National Archives.

Howe, Florence; Howard, Suzanne; and Strauss, Mary Jo Boehm. 1982. *Everywoman's Guide to Colleges and Universities*. Old Westbury, N.Y.: Feminist Press.

Hyde, William. 1979. *The Equity of the Distribution of Student Financial Aid*. Denver: Education Commission of the States. ED 176 664. 51 pp. MF–$1.00; PC–$7.29.

Jerue, Richard. November/December 1983. "Student Aid: Good Public Policy." *AGB Reports* 5: 4–8.

Johnson, Linda Byrd, and Smith, Carol J. 1984. *Higher Education Opportunities for Minorities and Women: Annotated Selections*. Washington, D.C.: U.S. Department of Education, Office of Postsecondary Education.

Johnson, Robert. 1983. *The Role of Educational Debt in Consumers' Total Debt Structure*. Prepared for the National Commission on Student Financial Assistance. Lafayette, Ind.: Purdue University, Credit Research Center. ED 228 939. 57 pp. MF–$1.00; PC–$7.29.

Jones, Effie, and Montenago, Xenia. 1982. *Recent Trends in the Representation of Women and Minorities in School Administration and Problems in Documentation*. Arlington, Va.: American Association of School Administrators. ED 226 468. 40 pp. MF–$1.00; PC–$5.44.

Kerr, Clark. 1985. "The States and Higher Education: Changes Ahead." *State Government* 58(2): 32.

Klein, Susan S., ed. 1985. *Handbook for Achieving Sex Equity through Education*. Baltimore: Johns Hopkins University Press.

Klitgaard, Robert. 1985. *Choosing Elites*. New York: Basic Books.

Kolstad, Andrew. 1982. *Does College Pay? Wage Rates before and after Leaving School.* Washington, D.C.: U.S. Department of Education, National Center for Education Statistics.

Kozol, Jonathan. 1985. *Illiterate America.* Garden City, N.Y.: Anchor Press/Doubleday.

Kuch, Peter. 1978. *Predicting Default and Bankruptcy: Factors Affecting the Repayment Status of Student Loans.* Technical Paper 78–111. Washington, D.C.: U.S. Department of Education, Office of Planning, Budget, and Evaluation.

Lee, John. 1982a. *Data Sets Available for Postsecondary Education Policy Analysis.* Prepared for the National Commission on Student Financial Assistance. Washington, D.C.: Applied Systems Institute.

————. 1982b. *Study of Guaranteed Student Loan Default Rates.* Prepared for the National Commission on Student Financial Assistance. Washington, D.C.: Applied Systems Institute. ED 228 952. 135 pp. MF–$1.00; PC–$12.84.

————. 1983. *Changes in College Participation Rates and Student Financial Assistance, 1969, 1974, 1981.* Prepared for the National Commission on Student Financial Assistance. Washington, D.C.: Applied Systems Institute. ED 228 941. 66 pp. MF–$1.00; PC–$7.29.

Leslie, Larry L. 1977. *Higher Education Opportunity: A Decade of Progress.* AAHE-ERIC Higher Education Research Report No. 3. Washington, D.C.: American Association for Higher Education. ED 152 862. 97 pp. MF–$1.00; PC–$9.14.

————. 1982. *Student Financing.* Report presented as part of the NIE Higher Education Indicators project. NIE Contract 400-80-0109. Boulder, Colo.: National Center for Higher Education Management Systems. ED 246 820. 253 pp. MF–$1.00; PC–$22.51.

Lewis, Shelby, et al. 1985. "Achieving Sex Equity for Minority Women." In *Handbook for Achieving Sex Equity through Education,* edited by Susan S. Klein. Baltimore: Johns Hopkins University Press.

Lindgren, J. Ralph; Ota, Patti T.; Zirkel, Perry A.; and Van Gieson, Nan. 1984. *Sex Discrimination Law in Higher Education: The Lessons of the Past Decade.* ASHE-ERIC Higher Education Report No. 4. Washington, D.C.: Association for the Study of Higher Education. ED 252 169. 84 pp. MF–$1.00; PC–$9.14.

Litten, Larry H.; Sullivan, Daniel; and Brodigan, David L. 1983. *Applying Market Research in College Admissions.* New York: College Entrance Examination Board.

Lyke, Robert. 1976. "Commentary on Student Loan Defaults." In *Student Loans: Problems and Policy Alternatives,* edited by

Lois Rice. New York: College Entrance Examination Board. ED 143 244. 180 pp. MF–$1.00; PC–$17.79.

Mathews, Martha, and McCune, Shirley. 1974. *Complying with Title IX: Implementing Institutional Self-Evaluation.* Washington, D.C.: U.S. Department of Health, Education, and Welfare.

Maxwell, James P. 1984. "Changes in the Ability of Students and Parents to Finance Higher Education Expenses from 1980 to 1982." Paper presented at the 1984 Annual Meeting of the American Education Research Association, 25 April, New Orleans, Louisiana.

Michigan Department of Social Services. 1985. *Assistance Application/Redetermination.* Lansing: Author.

Michigan Higher Education Assistance Authority and Michigan Higher Education Loan Authority. 1985. *Annual Report.* Lansing: Author.

Miller, Holly. 1985. "On the Road with Miss America." *The Saturday Evening Post* 257 (4): 42–45.

Miller, Scott E. 1984. *The National Commission on Student Financial Assistance: A Summary of Its Recommendations.* Policy Brief. Washington, D.C.: American Council on Education. ED 240 920. 5 pp. MF–$1.00; PC–$3.59.

Moore, James W. 1983. "Purposes and Provisions of Federal Programs." In *Handbook of Student Financial Aid,* edited by Robert H. Fenske and Robert P. Huff. San Francisco: Jossey-Bass.

Moran, Mary. June 1983. "Student Financial Assistance: Private Initiatives." *American Education* 46: 42–52.

———. 1984a. *Student Financial Assistance: Next Steps to Improving Education and Economic Opportunity for Women.* ED 246 712. 179 pp. MF–$1.00; PC–$16.96.

———. 1984b. *Women and Student Aid: A Preliminary Assessment.* Policy Brief. Washington, D.C.: American Council on Education.

National Advisory Committee on Black Higher Education and Black Colleges and Universities. 1977. *Higher Education Equity: The Crisis of Appearance versus Reality.* First Annual Report. Washington, D.C.: U.S. Government Printing Office. ED 157 493. 72 pp. MF–$1.00; PC–$7.29.

———. 1980. *Target Date, 2000 AD: Goals for Achieving Higher Education Equity for Black Americans,* vol. 1. Washington, D.C.: U.S. Government Printing Office. ED 197 682. 80 pp. MF–$1.00; PC–$9.14.

National Association of Student Financial Aid Administrators. 1985a. *Student Financial Aid: Making a Lifetime of Difference.* Washington, D.C.: Author.

———. 1985b. "Title IV of the Higher Education Act of 1965: As Amended through January 1985." *NASFAA Federal Monitor* 103. Washington, D.C.: Author.

National Collegiate Athletic Association. 1985. *1983–84 Annual Reports of the National Collegiate Athletic Association*. Mission, Kans.: Author.

National Commission on Student Financial Assistance. August 1982. Transcripts of commission meeting in Washington, D.C. Washington, D.C.: National Archives.

———. 1983a. *Satisfactory Academic Progress Standards for Federal Student Aid Recipients*. Report No. 5. ED 228 957. 76 pp. MF–$1.00; PC–$9.14.

———. 1983b. *Signs of Trouble and Erosion: A Report on Graduate Education in America*. ED 239 546. 87 pp. MF–$1.00; PC–$9.14.

———. 1984. "Guaranty Agency Questionnaire." Washington, D.C.: Author. ED 234 732. 9 pp. MF–$1.00; PC–$3.59.

National Council of Higher Education Loan Programs. 1984. *Introduction to the Guaranteed Student Loan Program*. Washington, D.C. Author.

National Governors Association. 1985. *The Impact of Proposed Changes in Federal Student Financial Assistance Policy: The States' Perspective*. Washington, D.C.: Author.

National Institute of Independent Colleges and Universities. 1983. Tabulations of distribution of student aid by gender at independent institutions. Washington, D.C.: Author.

National Merit Scholarship Corporation. 1985. *Annual Report: 1983–84*. Evanston, Ill.: Author.

———.1986. *Annual Report: 1984–85*. Evanston, Ill.: Author.

National School Boards Association. May 1986. "Resolutions, Beliefs and Policies, and Constitution and Bylaws of the National School Boards Association." *School Board News*. Alexandria, Va.: Author.

National Student Aid Coalition. 1985. *Report of the Task Force on Student Earnings of the Committee on Needs Assessment and Delivery*. Phase I. Washington, D.C.: Author.

National Student Nurses Association. 1985. *The Financial Aid Survey*. New York: Author.

National Urban League. 1984. *The State of Black America, 1984*. New York: Author.

*NCAA* v. *Califano,* 622 F.2d 1382 (10th Cir. 1980).

Newman, Frank. 1971. *Report on Higher Education*. Washington, D.C.: U.S. Government Printing Office. ED 049 718. 136 pp. MF–$1.00; PC–$13.26.

———. 1973. *The Second Newman Report: National Policy and*

*Higher Education.* Report of a Special Task Force to the Secretary of Health, Education, and Welfare. Washington, D.C.:
U.S. Government Printing Office. ED 090 828. 251 pp. MF–
$1.00; PC–$23.34.

Nolfi, George. 1983. *The Study of the Impact of Federal Student
Financial Aid Policies on State Decisions.* Prepared for the
National Commission on Student Financial Assistance. ED 234
731. 269 pp. MF–$1.00; PC–$22.51.

Olinsky, Arlene. 1983. *An Analysis of Financial Aid Utilization
by New York State Students, 1981–82.* New York: New York
State Higher Education Services Corporation.

O'Neill, Joseph P. 1984. *Corporate Tuition Aid Programs: A
Directory of College Financial Aid for Employees at America's
Largest Corporations.* Princeton, N.J.: Conference University
Press. ED 249 911. 329 pp. MF–$1.00; PC not available EDRS.

Osman, David S. 1982. "Status of Defaults and Collections under
the Guaranteed Student Loan and National Direct Student
Loan Programs." Policy Brief. Washington, D.C.: Congressional Research Service, Education and Public Welfare
Division.

Ostar, Allan W. 1976. *The Value of a College Education.* Washington, D.C.: American Association of State Colleges and Universities. ED 131 761. 10 pp. MF–$1.00; PC–$3.59.

Pallas, Aaron M., and Alexander, Karl L. 1983. "Sex Differences
in Quantitative SAT Performance: New Evidence on the Differential Coursework Hypothesis." *American Educational
Research Journal* 20 (2): 165–82.

Penner, Rudolph. 1984. Testimony before the Subcommittee on
Postsecondary Education, U.S. House of Representatives, 99th
Congress.

Peterson, Karen, and Rosco, Bruce. 1983. "Factors Influencing
Selection of Major by College Females." *College Student Journal* 17 (1): 32–33.

Project on the Status and Education of Women. 1980. *Campus
Child Care: A Challenge for the 80's.* Washington, D.C.: Asso-
ciation of American Colleges. ED 187 255. 15 pp. MF–$1.00;
PC–$3.59.

Rashkow, Ilona. 1976. *Veterans' Educational Benefits: 1944–
1976.* Washington, D.C.: Congressional Research Service.

Rees, Mina. 1976. "The Graduate Education of Women." In
*Women in Higher Education,* edited by W. Todd Furniss and
Patricia A. Graham. Washington, D.C.: American Council on
Education.

Renz, Loren. 1985. *The Foundation Directory,* 10th ed. New
York: The Foundation Center.

Rhodes Scholarship Trust. 1983. *Oxford and the Rhodes Scholarships*. Claremont, Cal.: Pamona College.

Rice, Lois, ed. 1976. *Student Loans: Problems and Policy Alternatives*. New York: College Entrance Examination Board. ED 143 244. 180 pp. MF–$1.00; PC–$17.79.

Rich, Spencer. 15 May 1985. "One-Parent Families Found to Increase Sharply in U.S.: Trend Affecting Blacks and Whites." *The Washington Post*.

Rix, Sara, and Stone, Anne. 1983. *Reductions and Realities: How the Federal Budget Affects Women*. Prepared for the Congressional Caucus on Women's Issues. Washington, D.C.: Women's Research and Education Institute.

Rosen, David Paul. 1983. *Resolving the Contradictions of Federal Public Assistance and College Opportunity Policies*. Prepared for the National Commission on Student Financial Assistance. ED 228 971. 47 pp. MF–$1.00; PC–$5.44.

Rosenfeld, Rachel A., and Hearn, James C. 1982. "Sex Differences in the Significance of Economic Resources for Choosing and Attending a College." In *The Undergraduate Woman: Issues in Education Equity,* edited by P. Perena. Lexington, Mass.: Lexington Books.

Sandler, Bernice R. 1986. *The Classroom Climate: A Chilly One for Women?* Washington, D.C.: Project on the Status and Education of Women. ED 215 628. 24 pp. MF–$1.00; PC–$3.59.

Sawyer, Kathy. 20 October 1983. "Job Bias Claim Settled by GM for $42 Million." *The Washington Post*.

Schlachter, Gail Ann. 1982. *Directory of Financial Aids for Women*. Santa Barbara, Cal.: Reference Service Press.

Shakeshaft, Carol. 1985. "Strategies for Overcoming the Barriers to Women in Educational Administration." In *Handbook for Achieving Sex Equity through Education,* edited by Susan S. Klein. Baltimore: Johns Hopkins University Press.

Shavlik, Donna L. 1984. *Senior Women Administrators in Higher Education: A Decade of Change, 1975–1984*. Washington, D.C.: American Council on Education.

Spero, Abby. 1985. *In America and in Need: Immigrant, Refugee, and Entrant Women*. U.S. Department of Labor contract number J-9-M-4-0065. Washington, D.C.: American Association of Community and Junior Colleges. ED 256 407. 189 pp. MF–$1.00; PC–$17.79.

Stampen, Jacob O. 1985. *Student Aid and Public Higher Education: Recent Changes*. Madison: University of Wisconsin.

Stanley, David T., and Girth, Marjorie. 1971. *Bankruptcy: Problem, Process, Reform*. Washington, D.C.: The Brookings Institution.

State Council of Higher Education for Virginia. 1982. *Responses of Other States to Reductions in Federal Student Assistance Programs: An Overview*. Richmond, Va.: Author.

Stelk, Kristen. 1983. *Student Aid Information: A Summary of Research and Public Policy Recommendations*. Prepared for the National Commission on Student Financial Assistance.

Thorndill, Steven. Spring 1983. "Some Insights into Computerized Scholarship Search Service." *Journal of Student Financial Aid* 13: 25–30.

Tierney, Michael L. 1982. *Trends in College Participation Rates*. Boulder, Colo.: National Center for Higher Education Management Systems. ED 246 819. 110 pp. MF–$1.00; PC–$11.41.

U.S. Congress. 1977. *Oversight Hearings on All Forms of Federal Student Financial Assistance*. Oversight hearings before the Subcommittee on Postsecondary Education, Committee on Education and Labor, U.S. House of Representatives. Washington, D.C.: U.S. Government Printing Office. ED 147 944. 728 pp. MF–$4.66; PC not available EDRS.

———. 1980a. *Conference Report to Accompany H.R. 5192: The Education Amendments of 1980*. U.S. House of Representatives, Ninety-sixth Congress, Second session. Washington, D.C.: U.S. Government Printing Office.

———. 1980b. *Federal Student Assistance: Issues and Options*. Washington, D.C.: Congressional Budget Office. ED 187 272. 90 pp. MF–$1.00; PC–$9.56.

———. 1983. *Education Quality and Federal Policy*. Hearings before the Task Force on Education and Employment, Committee on the Budget, U.S. House of Representatives. Serial No. TF4-5. Washington, D.C.: U.S. Government Printing Office.

———. 1984a. *Families and Child Care: Improving the Options*. A Report by the Select Committee on Children, Youth, and Families, U.S. House of Representatives. Washington, D.C.: U.S. Government Printing Office. ED 252 308. 184 pp. MF–$1.00; PC–$17.79.

———. 1984b. *Student Loan Consolidation*. Joint hearings before the Subcommittee on Postsecondary Education, Committee on Education and Labor, U.S. House of Representatives, and the Subcommittee on Education, Arts, and Humanities, Committee on Labor and Human Resources, U.S. Senate. Washington, D.C.: U.S. Government Printing Office.

U.S. Department of Commerce, Bureau of the Census. 1981. *Current Population Reports*. Population Characteristics, Series P-20, Number 362. Washington, D.C.: U.S. Government Printing Office.

U.S. Department of Education. 1979. "Revision of Policy Interpretations: Title IX and Intercollegiate Athletics." Washington, D.C.: Office for Civil Rights.

———1981. *Guidance for the Analysis of Student Financial Assistance in Determining Compliance with Title VI of the Civil Rights Act of 1964 and Title IX of the Education Amendments of 1972.* Washington, D.C.: Office for Civil Rights.

———. 1982. *Status of National Direct Student Loan Defaults as of June 30, 1982.* Institutional Listing. Washington, D.C.: Office of Student Financial Assistance.

———. 1983. "The High School and Beyond Data." 83-9-8. Washington, D.C.: National Center for Education Statistics, Longitudinal Studies Branch.

———. 1984a. *Annual Evaluation Report: Fiscal Year 1983.* Washington, D.C.: Office of Planning, Budget, and Evaluation. ED 240 747. 467 pp. MF–$1.00; PC–$37.72.

———. 1984b. *Application for Federal Student Aid: 1984–85 School Year.* Washington, D.C.: Office of Student Financial Assistance.

———. 1984c. *The Condition of Education.* Washington, D.C.: National Center for Education Statistics. ED 246 521. 231 pp. MF–$1.00; PC–$20.66.

———. 1984d. *Fall Enrollment in Colleges and Universities: 1982.* Washington, D.C.: National Center for Education Statistics.

———. 1984e. "Institutional Characteristics of Colleges and Universities. Higher Education General Information Survey." Data tape on institutional characteristics for 1983–84. Washington, D.C.: National Center for Education Statistics.

———. 1984f. *Justifications of Appropriation Estimates for Committees on Appropriations: Fiscal Year 1984,* vol. 2. Washington, D.C.: Office of Planning, Budgeting, and Evaluation.

———. 1984g. *Nationally Recognized Accrediting Agencies and Associations.* Washington, D.C.: Division of Eligibility and Agency Evaluation, Office of Postsecondary Education.

———. 1984h. *The Progress of an Agenda: A First Report from the Study Group on the Conditions of Excellence in American Higher Education.* Washington, D.C.: National Institute of Education. ED 244 577. 30 pp. MF–$1.00; PC–$5.44.

———. 1984i. *Semi-Annual Report of the Inspector General.* Washington, D.C.: Office of the Inspector General.

———. 1985a. *Campus-Based Programs.* Report No. 86-1. Notification to Members of Congress Regarding P.L. 89–329, the Higher Education Act of 1965, as amended. Washington, D.C.: Office of Student Financial Assistance.

———. 1985b. *The Student Guide: Five Federal Financial Aid Programs*. Washington, D.C.: Office of the Secretary.

———. 1986. *Education Department Recovers $116 Million from Student Loan Defaulters*. Washington, D.C.: Office of Public Affairs.

U.S. Department of Labor. 1984. *Time of Change: 1983 Handbook on Women Workers*. Washington, D.C.: Office of the Secretary, Women's Bureau.

———. 1985. *The United Nations Decade for Women, 1976–1985: Employment in the United States*. Washington, D.C.: Office of the Secretary, Women's Bureau.

U.S. Supreme Court. 1983. *"Grove City College v. Bell."* In *U.S. Supreme Court Oral Arguments,* vol. 5. Case nos. 82–766 to 82–849.

University of California. 15 November 1984. Press Release. Berkeley: University of California, Office of the President.

———. 19 June 1985. "Percent and Percentage Change of Minorities and Women within Federal Occupational Categories for Management and Staff." Press Release. Berkeley: University of California, Office of the President.

Van Dusen, William D., and Higginbotham, Hal F. 1984. *The Financial Aid Profession at Work: A Report on the 1983 Survey of Undergraduate Needs Analysis Policies, Practices, and Procedures*. Sponsored by the College Scholarship Service, the College Board, and the National Association of Student Financial Aid Administrators. New York: College Entrance Examination Board.

Webster, Bryce, and Perry, Robert L. 1983. *The Complete Social Security Handbook*. New York: Dodd, Mead & Co.

Weinberg, Steve. 1981. *Trade Secrets of Washington Journalists: How to Get the Facts about What's Going on in Washington*. Washington, D.C.: Acropolis Books.

Weitzman, Lenore. 1985. *The Divorce Revolution*. Stanford, Cal.: Stanford University.

Westervelt, Esther. 1975. *Barriers to Women's Participation in Postsecondary Education: A Review of Research and Commentary as of 1973–1974*. Washington, D.C.: National Center for Education Statistics. ED 111 256. 76 pp. MF–$1.00; PC–$9.56.

The White House. 1984. *Employer Options to Support Working Families: An Executive Summary for Chief Executive Officers*. Washington, D.C.: The White House, Office of Private Sector Initiatives.

Williams, Malaine Reeves, and Kent, Laura. 1982. *Blacks in Higher Education: Access, Choice, and Attainment*. Los Angeles: Higher Education Research Institute.

Wilms, Wellford. 1983. *Proprietary Vocational Schools: A Significant Sector of American Postsecondary Education*. Prepared for the National Commission on Student Financial Assistance. ED 228 942. 32 pp. MF–$1.00; PC–$5.44.

# INDEX

## A

AASA (see American Association of School Administrators)

Academic credentials: significance, 7

Access to postsecondary education
       equity issues, 40–41
       loan burden, 13
       low tuition factor, 4
       minority women, 32–33
       versus choice, 56

Accountability in aid distribution, 40, 57

Accrediting agencies, 75–76

ACT (see American College Testing)

Administrator leadership, 69–70

Admissions counselors, 36

Advanced training opportunities, 28

AFDC (see Aid to Families with Dependent Children)

Aid distribution
       by gender, 46–48, 91
       per recipient, 61, 89–90

Aid to Families with Dependent Children (AFDC), 24, 25, 30, 51, 72

Airline industry, 29

Allocation of aid, 60

American Association of School Administrators (AASA), 60

American Bar Association, 76

American College Testing (ACT) program, 17

American Council on Education, 70

American Federation of Teachers, 76

American Library Association, 76

American Medical Association, 76

American Optometric Association, 76

American University, 4

Arkansas State Board for Vocational Education, 76

Armed services recruitment, 70

Assessment of financial need, 33–35

Assistantships, 26–28

Athletic scholarships, 40, 45, 63–65

Awards
       average GSL, 45, 49
       average NDSL, 54–55
       average Pell Grant, 56
       average SEOG, 59
       average work study programs, 52–53
       total, 61

## B

Bachelor's degrees, 5, 66

Banking: on-campus, 73

College Scholarship Service, 81
College Work Study program, 22, 25, 30, 36, 45, 51, 53, 69, 72
Community colleges
     female enrollment, 2, 5, 19
     loan award regulations, 55
     low tuition/access, 2–3
Computer-assisted scholarship searches, 37
Computer sciences
     assistantships, 27
     enrollment, 5
     scholarships, 17
Confidentiality factor, 40, 79
Congressional action, 69
Cooperative education, 67, 72
Cooperative Institutional Research Program (CIRP), 44
Corporate benefits, 29–30, 45, 75, 78
Council of Economic Advisors, 81
Counseling: financial, 73
Course credit for aid eligibiity, 74
Court litigation, 9, 79–80
Credit card debt, 49
Credit unions, 73
Cultural factors in career choice, 28
CWS (see College Work Study)


**D**

Databases of financial aid information, 44, 81
Day care (see Child care)
Debt Collection Act of 1982, 15
Debts (see Loans/debt)
Defaults (see Loans/defaults)
Definition of financial need, 43
Departmental autonomy in awards, 26
Dependent students: male vs. female participation rates, 6
Disability payments, 24
Discriminatory practice continuation, 79–80
Displaced homemakers, 18
Divorce
     college degree litigation factor, 9
     loan burden/bankruptcy, 14, 15
     standard of living, 19
Doctoral degrees, 5, 27, 28
Dole, Robert, 75
Dole Foundation for Employment of Persons with Disabilities, 75

Graduate Record Exam, 17
Grants
    in-aid, 65
    institutional expenditures, 53
    insufficient for women, 49
    job training, 66
    state, 60–63
    total average, 11
GRE (see Graduate Record Exam)
Greene, Edith, 41
Grove City College v. Bell, 37, 38, 79
GSL (see Guaranteed Student Loans)
Guaranteed Student Loans (GSL), 13, 22, 30, 34, 45, 49, 51, 69, 77
Guidance counselor role, 37


**H**

Handicapped women, 31
HEAL (see Health Education Assistance Loans)
Health Education Assistance Loans (HEAL), 13
Health Profession Student Loans (HPSL), 13
High-income women, 49
High School and Beyond Survey, 44
High school—college cooperation, 69, 70–71
High school students
    dropout rates, 7
    female participation in advanced courses, 18
    targeted information, 36–37
Higher Education Act of 1980, 66
Hispanic women, 19
Home responsibility (see also Child care), 29
House Subcommittee on Postsecondary Education, 41
HPSL (see Health Profession Student Loans)


**I**

Illiteracy, 32
Independent students, 18–22, 35
Industry
    corporate benefits, 29–30
    joint effort, minority graduate students, 33
Information dissemination, 36–37, 70–71, 73, 78
Information needs, 81–82
Institutional "Office of Veterans' Affairs," 66
Institutional practices, 69–76
Internal Revenue Service (IRS), 76, 81
Internships, 28, 40
IRS (see Internal Revenue Service)

## J

## L

## M

---

New York state: financial aid, 22
New York University: access to women, 4
Newman Task Force, 41
Newspapers: student, 73
Nondegree coursework, 74
Nontraditional occupations, 67
North Central Association of Colleges and Schools, 76
NSL (see Nursing Student Loans)
Nursing Student Loans (NSL), 13
Nursing students, 77

**O**

O'Neill, Thomas P., 75
Occupational distribution, 35
Office for Civil Rights, 37, 38, 64
Office of Management and Budget, 81
Office of Vocational and Adult Education, 66, 67
Oklahoma State Regents for Higher Education, 76
One-parent families (see Single parents)
Oregon: women's programs, 62
Out-of-state students, 49
Outreach programs, 73–74

**P**

Parent Loans for Undergraduate Students, 13
Parents (see also Single parents): financial contribution, 34
Part-time jobs, 17
Part-time students, 19, 22–24
    child care cost factor, 31
    eligibility for aid, 59
    growth, 35
Participation rates
    dependent students, 6
    GSL, 45, 49, 50
    NDSL, 54–55
    overall, by socioeconomic status, 2
    Pell Grant, 56
    SEOG, 59
    work study programs, 52–53
Partnerships
    corporations and colleges, 78
    schools and colleges, 70–71
Paying for college, 43–67, 92–94
Pell, Claiborne, 55
Pell Grants, 30, 34, 37, 38, 45, 55–57, 59, 80, 81
Perkins (Carl T.) Vocational Education Act of 1984, 67

---

Reentry students
    college, 18
    high school, 7
Regulatory restrictions (see also Eligibility)
    GSLs, 51
    Pell Grants, 57
Remedial courses: math and science, 6, 43, 74
Research assistantships, 27, 28, 71
Retail industry, 29
Retraining needs, 35
Rhodes Scholarship, 17
Richardson, Elliot, 41
Robb, Charles, 60
Rural area dropout prevention, 75

**S**

St. Louis University, 4
Sallie Mae, 77, 78, 81
Sarah Lawrence College, 4
SAT (see Scholastic Aptitude Test)
Scholarships
    academic, 65
    athletic, 40, 45, 63–65
    corporate, 75
    merit, 16–18, 40, 53
    military, 45, 65–66
    women's, 73
Scholastic Aptitude Test (SAT), 17, 18, 99
School board leadership, 70-71
School superintendent leadership, 70–71
Sciences
    assistantships, 27
    cultural influences, 28
    high school advanced courses, 18
    remedial courses, 6, 43, 74
    scholarships, 16, 17
Selecting a college, 1–3
Selective colleges, 7
Self-assessment (institutional), 78–80
Self-help programs, 22
SEOG (see Supplemental Educational Opportunity Grants)
Sex discrimination prohibition, 62
Sex equity: athletics, 65
Single parents, 18, 19, 28
Social security benefits, 24, 25
Socialization of graduate students, 27–28
Source of income calculations, 25

Southern Illinois University-Edwardsville, 74
Southern Methodist University, 4
Special Services Grants for Disadvantaged Students program, 32
Spouse financial support, 9, 34
Sputnik, 53
SSIG (see State Student Incentive Grants)
Staff development cost reimbursement, 30, 78
Standard-of-living allowances, 25
State governors' role, 60
State scholarships/grants, 45, 60–63
State Student Incentive Grants (SSIG), 36, 62–63
Student aid office vs. student aid program, 40
Student loan programs (see Loans)
   Summer employment, 34, 51, 52, 53, 65, 71, 72
Supplemental Educational Opportunity Grants (SEOG), 22, 45,
   53, 57–60, 60
Supplemental Social Security Income, 24
Supreme Court, 37, 38, 39, 40, 80

**T**
Tax credits: child care, 30, 78
Teachers
   loans, 53
   recruitment, 66
Teaching assistantships, 27, 28, 71
Teenage mothers, 31, 32
Test performance, 18
Time to complete degree, 6, 26
Title III, Higher Education Act, 32
Title IV, Higher Education Act, 69
Title IX, Education Amendments of 1972, 5, 37–41, 63–65, 78–80
Title VI, Civil Rights Act of 1964, 38
Title VIII, Higher Education Act of 1980, 66
Transfer students, 6, 43, 74
Transportation costs, 31, 56
Travel subsidy, 28
Trends
   distribution in financial aid by gender, 44, 46–48
   economic, 9–11
Trust funds, 75
Trustee responsibility, 70
Tuition
   corporate benefits, 29–30, 78
   costs, 1
   reduced fee, 74
   waivers, 53
Two-year colleges (see Community colleges)

# ASHE-ERIC HIGHER EDUCATION REPORTS

Starting in 1983, the Association for the Study of Higher Education assumed cosponsorship of the Higher Education Reports with the ERIC Clearinghouse on Higher Education. For the previous 11 years, ERIC and the American Association for Higher Education prepared and published the reports.

Each report is the definitive analysis of a tough higher education problem, based on a thorough research of pertinent literature and institutional experiences. Report topics, identified by a national survey, are written by noted practitioners and scholars with prepublication manuscript reviews by experts.

Eight monographs (10 monographs before 1985) in the ASHE-ERIC Higher Education Report series are published each year, available individually or by subscription. Subscription to eight issues is $60 regular; $50 for members of AERA, AAHE, and AIR; $40 for members of ASHE. (Add $7.50 outside the United States.)

Prices for single copies, including 4th class postage and handling, are $10.00 regular and $7.50 for members of AERA, AAHE, AIR, and ASHE ($7.50 regular and $6.00 for members for 1983 and 1984 reports, $6.50 regular and $5.00 for members for reports published before 1983). If faster 1st class postage is desired for U.S. and Canadian orders, add $.75 for each publication ordered; overseas, add $4.50. For VISA and MasterCard payments, include card number, expiration date, and signature. Orders under $25 must be prepaid. Bulk discounts are available on orders of 15 or more reports (not applicable to subscriptions). Order from the Publications Department, Association for the Study of Higher Education, One Dupont Circle, Suite 630, Washington, D.C. 20036, 202/296-2597. Write for a publication list of all the Higher Education Reports available.

### 1986 Higher Education Reports

1. Post-tenure Faculty Evaluation: Threat or Opportunity?
   *Christine M. Licata*

2. Blue Ribbon Commissions and Higher Education: Changing Academe from the Outside
   *Janet R. Johnson and Laurence R. Marcus*

3. Responsive Professional Education: Balancing Outcomes and Opportunities
   *Joan S. Stark, Malcolm A. Lowther, and Bonnie M.K. Hagerty*

4. Increasing Students' Learning: A Faculty Guide to Reducing Stress among Students
   *Neal A. Whitman, David C. Spendlove, and Claire H. Clark*

5. Student Financial Aid and Women: Equity Dilemma?
   *Mary Moran*

### 1985 Higher Education Reports

1. Flexibility in Academic Staffing: Effective Policies and Practices
   *Kenneth P. Mortimer, Marque Bagshaw, and Andrew T. Masland*

2. Associations in Action: The Washington, D.C., Higher Education Community
   *Harland G. Bloland*

---

**1983 Higher Education Reports**

1. The Path to Excellence: Quality Assurance in Higher Education
   *Laurence R. Marcus, Anita O. Leone, and Edward D. Goldberg*

2. Faculty Recruitment, Retention, and Fair Employment: Obligations and Opportunities
   *John S. Waggaman*

3. Meeting the Challenges: Developing Faculty Careers
   *Michael C. T. Brookes and Katherine L. German*

4. Raising Academic Standards: A Guide to Learning Improvement
   *Ruth Talbott Keimig*

5. Serving Learners at a Distance: A Guide to Program Practices
   *Charles E. Feasley*

6. Competence, Admissions, and Articulation: Returning to the Basics in Higher Education
   *Jean L. Preer*

7. Public Service in Higher Education: Practices and Priorities
   *Patricia H. Crosson*

8. Academic Employment and Retrenchment: Judicial Review and Administrative Action
   *Robert M. Hendrickson and Barbara A. Lee*

9. Burnout: The New Academic Disease
   *Winifred Albizu Meléndez and Rafael M. de Guzmán*

10. Academic Workplace: New Demands, Heightened Tensions
    *Ann E. Austin and Zelda F. Gamson*

# NOTES

# NOTES

# NOTES

# NOTES